Reader's Digest · National Trust

Nature Notebooks

RIVER, WETLAND AND LOWLAND BIRDS

Reader's Digest · National Trust

Nature Notebooks

RIVER, WETLAND AND LOWLAND BIRDS

Published by The Reader's Digest Association Limited, London,
in association with The National Trust

Additional editorial work by Duncan Petersen Publishing Limited,
5 Botts Mews, London W2 5AG.
Typesetting by Modern Reprographics Limited, Hull,
North Humberside.
Separations by Modern Reprographics Limited, (covers)
and Mullis Morgan Limited, London (duplicate film)
Printed by Everbest Printing Company Limited, Hong Kong

The illustration on the cover is by Michael Woods.

CONTENTS

Using This Book	6-7
Identifying Birds: Basic Fieldcraft	8-10
The Birds	11-95
The Sites	96-119
Understanding Birds and Recording Techniques	120-22
Glossary	123-24
Index	125-26
Acknowledgements	127

Using this book

Britain used to enjoy a great wealth of river, wetland and lowland habitats; their decline in recent years, from a variety of factors, but mostly from the activities of man, has received much publicity. The fascinating range of birds these habitats support is, of course, under threat as well, so it is particularly useful to the bird-watcher that a book such as this brings together not only an identification guide to familiar river, wetland and lowland birds, but also lists sites where they can be seen.

The field guide section, pages 12-95, works hand-in-hand with the sites gazetteer, pages 96-119 by means of the panel on each field guide page. The panel includes a brief general note on each species – often describing the bird's nest. A nest affords the naturalist an excellent opportunity for watching and identifying birds, but we would stress how essential it is not to approach too close.

Below the caption we list a sequence of numbers directing you to sites described in the gazetteer, in all of which you have an excellent chance of seeing the bird in question. They are not the *only* sites in the book where you will see it, but they are the most interesting ones. Equally, you will find some species cross-referenced to a site, but not mentioned in the site description: this is because space in the gazetteer is restricted.

In certain cases, comparisons are made between the appearance or habits of a river, lowland or wetland bird and those of a bird not included in this book. This is for the benefit of those who may possess the two other books in this series: *Garden and Woodland Birds* and *Seaside and Moorland Birds*.

These companion titles contain birds which also inhabit rivers, wetland and lowland, and for this reason are well worth owning along with this book. However, their river, wetland and lowland habitats are rather more specialized in nature, occurring mainly in association with coastal, moorland, upland, garden and woodland habitats; the birds featured in this book are generally regular river, wetland and lowland species; and likewise the sites described in the gazetteer are 'mainstream' locations for these species.

One particularly important and interesting type of habitat occurring only in this title is lowland heath.

The selection of species
The 84 birds chosen for the field guide section are by no means all the river, wetland and lowland birds that can be seen in Britain; however, they are a representative selection of the most familiar of such species, and they are the most likely to be seen by the visitor without local knowledge. Among them are a fair sprinkling of uncommon birds, but also birds which, though rare on a nationwide basis, can easily be seen if you visit the site which specializes in them. Where no specific sites are mentioned, the bird is either so common that it can be seen at the majority of sites, or so rare that its nesting areas are deliberately kept secret.

The selection of sites
The places described for bird-watching in the gazetteer section are, in England and Wales, mainly National Trust property. They have the excellent

advantage of generally easy access, though it should also be realized that much of the land is not for the public to roam freely. Viewing is in many places from roads only, or from footpaths and tracks which are public rights of way. For this reason, a large scale map such as the Ordnance Survey Landranger series (scale 1:50 000) is extremely useful since it shows footpaths which are public rights of way.

The Scottish and Irish sites are in some cases managed by the National Trust for Scotland; otherwise they are Nature Reserves or Bird Sanctuaries to which the public generally has easy access – without membership of an organization or possessing a special permit. In addition to the National Trust sites in England and Wales, there are also featured a number of first-class properties owned or managed by other bodies: these are intended to make the coverage more comprehensive, in terms of geographical spread and of species.

The panel for notes
The space at the foot of each colour plate on pages 12-95 is a convenient introduction to the excellent – some would say essential – habit of making notes of bird observations. Individual headings are given for all the most important types of information needing to be logged when seeing a bird: location, time of day, weather, behaviour, and so on; but most important of all is the blank space left free for a sketch. However feeble you believe your artistic efforts may be, they are always worth making: a sketch forces you to recall, or to note specific aspects of a bird in detail.

The colour plates

The superb bird illustrations on pages 12-95 give you not only close-up, but also distant views of every species, and this is of course invaluable.

There are sometimes marked differences between the plumages of males and females of the same species, or between their winter and summer or adult and juvenile plumages. All the main plumage variations which occur during a bird's stay in Britain are illustrated.

The distribution maps

The map on each colour plate shows you when and where you are most likely to see the species. The time of year when you see a bird, or the part of Britain where you see it, can be useful clues.

Red dots show the sites of breeding colonies.
Red shading shows the usual breeding range of summer visitors.
Green shows the usual breeding range of species present in Britain all year round.
Blue shows the areas where a species is found in winter.
Shading indicates where passage migrants occur – those species which stop in Britain while moving to or from breeding or wintering grounds.

THE NATIONAL TRUST AND ITS WORK

The National Trust, a private charity founded in 1895, could be said to be the oldest conservation organization in the country. As well as caring for historic houses, castles and gardens, it owns 500,000 acres of land throughout England, Wales and Northern Ireland. It acquired its first Nature Reserve, Wicken Fen, as early as 1895, and by 1910 had 13 properties of particular wildlife value. It now owns some 90 Nature Reserves, over 400 Sites of Special Scientific Interest (SSSIs) and many other properties of great interest, not only for birds, but for a great range of animal and plant communities.

The National Trust for Scotland, a separate organization, but with similar aims and objectives, was established in 1931 and owns 100,000 acres, including some of the finest mountain and coastal scenery in Scotland.

The Royal Society for the Protection of Birds (RSPB) and the Royal Society for Nature Conservation (RSNC) which, like the National Trusts, are charities with no direct government funding, have also been actively involved in wildlife conservation for many decades. The RSPB was founded in 1889 and manages over a 100 reserves covering 130,000 acres. The RSNC, established in 1912, acts as a national association for 46 Nature Conservation Trusts which between them manage over 1,600 nature reserves covering 1,120,000 acres.

The loss of lowland wildlife habitats due to intensification of agriculture, expansion of towns and roads, new power stations, airports and waste-tips, regulation for water-supplies and many other factors has received much publicity in the last few years. In the face of this alarming decline, the National Trust has a very important role to play.

The main threat to the birdlife of Britain's rivers is the loss of bankside nesting habitat – the sheltering bushes and overhanging trees and the adjacent marshy grassland so important for feeding. Where the National Trust owns the banks it can liaise with the Water Authorities to make sure that disturbance is minimized, and can also ensure that bankside vegetation is retained.

One of the most threatened of the lowland habitats in Britain, and one with a particularly large assemblage of specifically associated plants and animals, is lowland heath.

During long hot, dry periods, the visitor can be a serious problem on heaths, as accidental summer fires, which burn deep into the peat, can destroy the heather and much of the less mobile wildlife. National Trust wardens spend much extra time patrolling on summer weekends, watching for fire.

Visits to even a small proportion of the sites listed in this book should serve to emphasise the great importance of our remaining semi-natural lowland habitats, and their enormous variety of birds.

Katherine Hearn,
Assistant Adviser on Conservation,
The National Trust.

Identifying Birds: Basic Fieldcraft

To identify birds successfully, you need to concentrate your powers of observation on several distinct aspects of a given species. Probably the two most important are distinguishing, or diagnostic, field marks, and relative size. The pictures and captions on pages 10 and 11 will help you get to grips with these basic concepts. Of course, you will also need to be aware of, and observe, overall plumage colour, bill shape and size, flight pattern, song and behaviour. Building up a working knowledge of these is largely a matter of experience; and of capitalizing on that experience by taking notes – see page 6.

But clearly, if you are too far away from the bird to see or hear it, all the ornithological knowledge in the world is of little practical value. You need, in addition, some skill in fieldcraft – the art of being in the right place at the right time. Its object is to get you close enough to make a positive identification, either on the spot, or later with the help of notes and a field guide.

There is no great mystery in fieldcraft – most of it is simple commonsense, and many of the techniques described below will be familiar to anyone who has spent time watching birds feeding in a garden or local park.

Fieldcraft starts before you even leave home on a bird-watching trip: time spent in planning and preparation is never wasted. Check the weather report: forecasts of rain or poor visibility could mean disappointment. Plan your journey so that, if possible, you arrive at your destination early – song is a valuable clue, and is at its loudest early in the day.

Before leaving you should also think about clothing and footwear suitable for the trip. Choose inconspicuous clothes in camouflage colours, rather than bright hues which attract attention. Try also to find clothing that doesn't rustle – some garments made from artificial fibre make a noise each time you move.

Take footwear that is suited to the terrain you are visiting: gum boots are ideal for wetland sites, but for long days walking over heath or farmland, there is no substitute for a pair of proper leather walking boots.

Though you can often identify a bird with the naked eye, binoculars make the process much easier. When choosing a pair, look for the two engraved numbers – such as 10 × 50. The smaller number indicates magnification; the larger number, the lens diameter, and thus the light-gathering power of the binoculars. For the novice bird-watcher, 8 × 30s are a sound first choice. They are easy to focus, gather sufficient light even for use at dusk, and are not too heavy to carry round all day. Before buying a pair, though, it is wise to try other people's binoculars and see which you prefer.

> Try to buy binoculars from a friendly, co-operative dealer, and ask him to let you compare the sharpness of different makes by focusing on, say, a sheet of newspaper pinned up 20 yards (18 m) away. Also compare brightness of image, weight, general handling and whether suited to the wearer of spectacles.

In the field

Once you are on the spot, it almost goes without saying that you should be as inconspicuous as possible. If you are visiting a small area, start by doing a brief survey of the site before choosing somewhere to settle down. On heath, for example, try to find a slight rise with cover of shrub or gorse: this can give excellent, uninterrupted views.

Being inconspicuous can mean literally concealing yourself in the shelter of a wall or fence, but you might be surprised at how little cover is needed to deceive a bird. The strong lines of a five-bar gate, for example, are often enough to disguise your human outline – provided you keep still.

If you plan to walk some distance, you'll want to get a move on, but more birds will be visible if you make regular stops, keeping still for five to ten minutes. In constant motion yourself, it is easy to miss the small movements in undergrowth that can alert you to the presence of birdlife. Additionally, birds are less frightened by static observers, and will come closer to you. If you suspect that there are birds around, but that they will not emerge from cover, try making a noise; but in the breeding season do not, for this may cause birds to abandon nests.

Timing

Few people enjoy getting up before dawn, but since the very early morning is such an important time for bird-watching, it makes sense to choose sites close to where you live for such expeditions. Several localities featured in the sites gazetteer lie within easy driving distance of major population centres; and indeed, London parks, with their lakes, can offer some interesting close views of water-birds, including the great crested grebe, whose spring-time courtship ritual is a wonder of bird behaviour.

Knowing what to look for is the key to success in identifying birds. The size, shape and colouring of a bird are the first and most obvious clues to its identity. But how it stands or moves, how it swims or flies, how it sings, feeds or approaches its mate – these and other aspects of its behaviour may be just as distinctive as its plumage. The time of year, and the place where the bird is seen, are also identification points. Some birds only visit Britain at particular times of the year, coming from breeding or wintering grounds that may be thousands of miles away. Other birds are so well adapted to life in a particular habitat that they are only rarely encountered outside it.

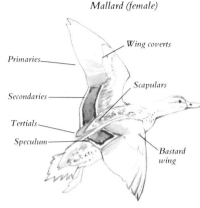

Mallard (female)

Primaries

Secondaries

Tertials

Speculum

Wing coverts

Scapulars

Bastard wing

Oystercatcher

Wing-bar

Rump

Terminal band

House sparrow (male)

Crown

Forehead

Ear coverts

Beak

Nape

Chin

Back

Throat

Breast

Rump

Upper tail coverts

Tail

Under tail coverts

Hind claw

Toes

Tarsus

Flanks

Belly

Supercilium

Eye-ring

Moustachial stripe

Reed bunting (female)

Naming the parts

Putting the right name to the parts of a bird is almost as important as naming the bird itself. For it provides a language in which to discuss birds with other birdwatchers, and it makes for quick and simple note-taking in the field.

Getting up early does not only reward you, in spring and summer, with the dawn chorus. There follows much foraging and nest-building activity among paired birds, which is generally easy to observe. By mid-morning, you will probably notice a lull in activity as the birds stop to rest or preen.

A similar pattern of behaviour is also noticeable in autumn when mixed flocks of finches sweep over arable land. The flocks form early in the morning to feed hungrily in stubble, in farmyards or at the edges of fields. Then follows a slack period lasting until the afternoon, when small parties of birds reassemble and fly directly to roost sites in thick scrub.

Larger-scale movements take place on a country-wide basis with the changing seasons, of course. The great influxes of migrant or passage wetland birds are the obvious examples; however, when planning bird trips, bear in mind, too, that even among resident species there is a great deal of movement generally south and west to more sheltered feeding grounds.

What size is it?

When an unfamiliar bird is seen, the first point to note is its size. The easiest way to fix this is by comparing it with a bird that is known. Measured from its bill tip to the tip of its tail, for instance, a house sparrow is 5¾ in. (14·5 cm), while a blackbird is nearly twice as long, at 10 in. (25 cm). The familiar mallard is twice as long again, at 23 in. (58 cm), while its frequent companion on the waters of rivers and lakes, the mute swan, is the largest of all British birds, at 60 in. (152 cm) in length. The shape of a bird can also be very distinctive. For instance, it may be slim and delicate like a wagtail, or plump and stocky like a wood-pigeon.

House sparrow
5¾ in. (14·5 cm)
Heavily built,
with thick bill.

Blackbird
10 in. (25 cm)
Sturdy; adult
male's bill yellow.

Pied wagtail
7 in. (18 cm)
Long and slender.

Black-headed gull
15 in. (38 cm)
Long, pointed wings.

Wood-pigeon
16 in. (40 cm)
Heavy bodied;
broad wings.

Mallard
23 in. (58 cm)
Stout bodied;
long wings.

Mute swan
60 in. (152 cm)
Long neck, curved
when not in flight.

Remember also that usually the nearer a stretch of water lies to the coast, the better the chance of seeing large numbers of different waders.

Song

Some of the most exciting habitats featured in this book are reed beds, and they illustrate especially well the usefulness of a little knowledge of bird song. Many of the smaller reed bed birds are skulkers, and the only way to locate them initially is by sound. Sound recordings (the RSPB sell one at a reasonable price) are of course the ideal way to gather a knowledge of bird song; but few people mistake the reeling sound of the grasshopper warbler – rather like a fishing line being drawn off a reel – even when hearing it for the first time. The same is true of the curious hissing sound and low growl of the woodcock when roding – its unique territorial flight made late on spring evenings around woodland edges. These are among the most memorable sounds you will hear on days out with this book.

THE BIRDS

An identification guide to 84 species

●

The species are grouped by family, starting with the
more primitive families and ending with the most
advanced species. For some basic advice on identifying
birds, see pages 8-10; for further information on bird
classification, see page 120.

●

If you already know the name of a species and want to
look it up, simply consult the index.

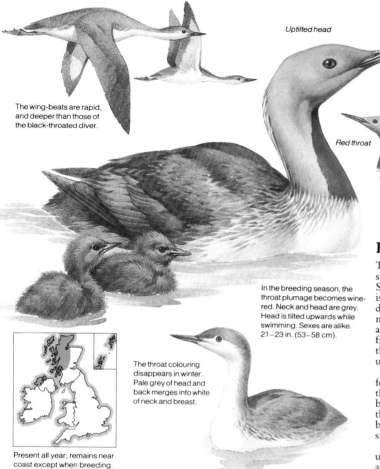

The wing-beats are rapid, and deeper than those of the black-throated diver.

Uptilted head

Red throat

A bird on the alert swims low in the water. Its throat-patch looks dark unless seen in a bright light.

In the breeding season, the throat plumage becomes wine-red. Neck and head are grey. Head is tilted upwards while swimming. Sexes are alike. 21–23 in. (53–58 cm).

The throat colouring disappears in winter. Pale grey of head and back merges into white of neck and breast.

Present all year; remains near coast except when breeding.

Sites Guide

The nest of the red-throated diver is usually a heap of moss or water plants, in offshore shallows or on land at the water's edge.

The species may be seen at site number: 1.

Red-throated diver *Gavia stellata*

The red-throated diver is a good swimmer both on or below the surface, and one of only four species of diver in the world. Superbly streamlined, neck outstretched and legs tucked back, it is also graceful in flight. Alas, like all divers, it is somewhat at a disadvantage on landing: its legs, so well adapted for swimming, are set far back on its body, giving the bird a most awkward gait. But so efficient is it under water that it can chase fish or scoop up shellfish as deep as 30 ft (9 m). And so fast is it on the surface that a courting bird may 'run' on the water, beating up spray with its wings.

Like other divers, the red-throated species loses its flight feathers in late summer, and is grounded until new ones grow – though it can still dive for food. It takes to the coast in winter but breeds on small Highland lochs, nesting in shallow water or near the shoreline, and usually laying two dark olive eggs, spotted or blotched blackish-brown. Chicks hatch in about four weeks, swim within 24 hours and fly at around six weeks.

A reedy cooing is the bird's most musical call. Country folk used to think the mewing wail of a courting bird heralded rain, and named it the 'rain goose'.

Location	Behaviour	Sketch
Date		
Time		
Weather	Field marks	
Call		

Little grebes take to the wing more than other grebes, often flying low over water.

Adult in breeding plumage has a red neck and a pale patch at inner end of bill. Female is duller than male. Young are very small, with striped head and back. 10–12 in. (25–30 cm).

Pale patch

Red neck

Winter plumage is much paler; dull brown above, buff and white below.

In summer adults often puff themselves up, both at rest and in some display postures.

Present all year; on fresh water with vegetation.

When alarmed, the little grebe submerges, with only its head showing.

SITES GUIDE

The little grebe builds its nest of water plants, often supported by a fallen branch in shallow water.

The species may be seen at sites numbers: 7, 13, 14, 16, 18, 23, 25, 27, 32, 37–39, 44, 45, 48, 54, 55.

Little grebe *Tachybaptus ruficollis*

From Buckingham Palace lake to the humblest farm pond, the little grebe – often called the dabchick – is the most widespread of its family in Britain as well as the smallest. It is at home in any still or slow-flowing fresh water that has a lush growth of vegetation. On large lakes it spends much of its time in the more sheltered, shallow bays with a thick growth of underwater plants.

If observed during its busy search for small fish or water insects, the bird looks like a small ball of feathers, diving frequently and bobbing up again. Sometimes, to make a deeper dive, it jumps up first and enters the water with a splash. The little grebe is more often identified by its trilling call, something like the whinny of a horse and rising and falling in volume and pitch over the space of a few seconds. Pairs prefer to keep to themselves, but on their favourite stretches of water the population may be so dense that they virtually breed in colonies.

Two, or sometimes three, clutches of four to six eggs are laid during the long breeding season. They are white, but soon stained by water-weed. Chicks hatch in about a month and quickly leave the nest, often carried on the parents' backs.

Location	Behaviour	Sketch
Date		
Time		
Weather	Field marks	
Call		

13

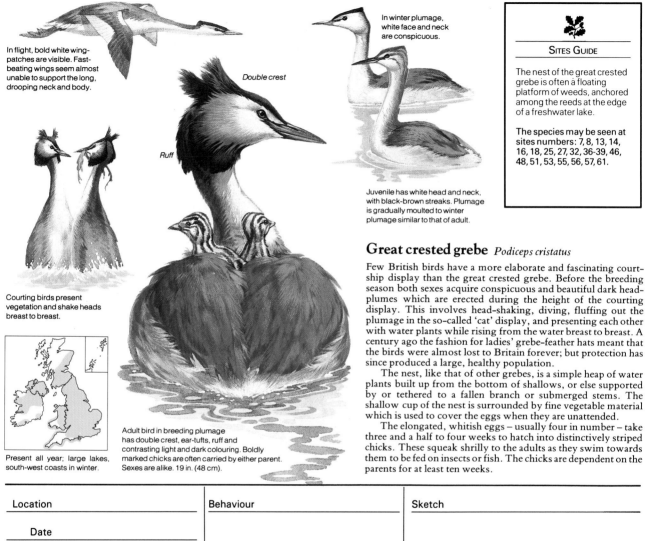

In flight, bold white wing-patches are visible. Fast-beating wings seem almost unable to support the long, drooping neck and body.

Double crest

In winter plumage, white face and neck are conspicuous.

Ruff

Juvenile has white head and neck, with black-brown streaks. Plumage is gradually moulted to winter plumage similar to that of adult.

Courting birds present vegetation and shake heads breast to breast.

Present all year; large lakes, south-west coasts in winter.

Adult bird in breeding plumage has double crest, ear-tufts, ruff and contrasting light and dark colouring. Boldly marked chicks are often carried by either parent. Sexes are alike. 19 in. (48 cm).

Sites Guide

The nest of the great crested grebe is often a floating platform of weeds, anchored among the reeds at the edge of a freshwater lake.

The species may be seen at sites numbers: 7, 8, 13, 14, 16, 18, 25, 27, 32, 36-39, 46, 48, 51, 53, 55, 56, 57, 61.

Great crested grebe *Podiceps cristatus*

Few British birds have a more elaborate and fascinating courtship display than the great crested grebe. Before the breeding season both sexes acquire conspicuous and beautiful dark head-plumes which are erected during the height of the courting display. This involves head-shaking, diving, fluffing out the plumage in the so-called 'cat' display, and presenting each other with water plants while rising from the water breast to breast. A century ago the fashion for ladies' grebe-feather hats meant that the birds were almost lost to Britain forever; but protection has since produced a large, healthy population.

The nest, like that of other grebes, is a simple heap of water plants built up from the bottom of shallows, or else supported by or tethered to a fallen branch or submerged stems. The shallow cup of the nest is surrounded by fine vegetable material which is used to cover the eggs when they are unattended.

The elongated, whitish eggs – usually four in number – take three and a half to four weeks to hatch into distinctively striped chicks. These squeak shrilly to the adults as they swim towards them to be fed on insects or fish. The chicks are dependent on the parents for at least ten weeks.

Location	Behaviour	Sketch
Date		
Time		
Weather	Field marks	
Call		

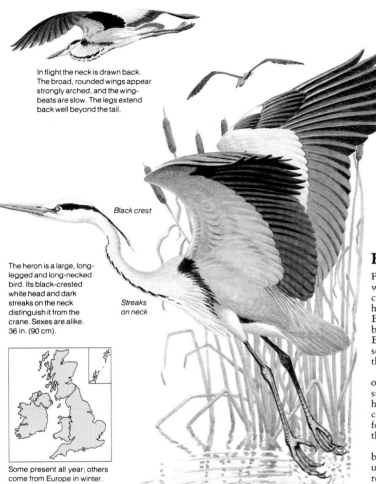

In flight the neck is drawn back. The broad, rounded wings appear strongly arched, and the wing-beats are slow. The legs extend back well beyond the tail.

Black crest

The heron is a large, long-legged and long-necked bird. Its black-crested white head and dark streaks on the neck distinguish it from the crane. Sexes are alike. 36 in. (90 cm).

Streaks on neck

Some present all year; others come from Europe in winter.

Heron *Ardea cinerea*

Poised alert and motionless in or beside shallow water, the watchful heron waits patiently for a fish or some other small creature to come within range of its dagger-sharp bill. Then the heron strikes, stabbing the prey and swallowing it whole. Besides fish, herons readily take small mammals and amphibians, reptiles, insects and even birds. The heron population of Britain fluctuates between 4,000 and 4,500 pairs, but falls after severe winters when frozen rivers and lakes deprive the birds of their main food.

Herons nest in colonies, or heronries, building in large trees or bushes, in reed-beds or on cliff edges. The nest is a large structure of sticks and twigs with a shallow, saucer-shaped hollow in the top. The same nest is used year after year, and consequently grows in size until it is several feet across. The female usually builds the nest and lays three, four or five eggs that are pale greenish-blue in colour.

The chicks which emerge are clad in long, sparse down, bristly on the crown, giving a comical crest-like effect. Keeping up an incessant, begging 'agagagagag' call, they are fed by regurgitation by both parents.

Location	Behaviour	Sketch
Date		
Time		
Weather	Field marks	
Call		

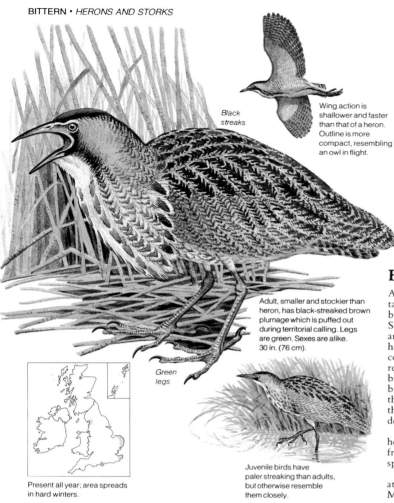

Black streaks

Wing action is shallower and faster than that of a heron. Outline is more compact, resembling an owl in flight.

Bitterns can climb tall reeds by grasping several at a time.

Adult, smaller and stockier than heron, has black-streaked brown plumage which is puffed out during territorial calling. Legs are green. Sexes are alike. 30 in. (76 cm).

Green legs

Present all year; area spreads in hard winters.

Juvenile birds have paler streaking than adults, but otherwise resemble them closely.

SITES GUIDE

The bittern's nest is built among reeds or sedge. It consists of fragments of waterside vegetation lined with finer matter.

The species may be seen at sites numbers: 2, 15, 28, 34, 36, 43.

Bittern *Botaurus stellaris*

At the beginning of the 19th century, bitterns were regarded as a table delicacy and special shoots were organised in the fens and broadlands of eastern England – as well as in Wales, southern Scotland and Ireland. The bird was then quite common in those areas. By the middle of the century, however, the population had collapsed as a result of the shoots, the activity of egg-collectors and drainage of the marshes. The last breeding was recorded in Norfolk in 1868. Then, at the start of this century, bitterns from the Continent began to recolonise Britain, and breeding recommenced in 1911. Despite some severe winters, the bittern population steadily increased and reached a peak in the 1950s. Since then a decline has set in, because of further destruction of suitable habitats.

The bittern's call is a deep, resonant 'boom', which may be heard as far as 1 mile away. Its generic name *Botaurus* is derived from the Latin *boatum tauri*, 'the bellowing of a bull', and in the spring its call resembles the distant lowing of a cow.

In the breeding season, four to six olive-brown eggs are laid at two to three day intervals and are incubated by the hen. Meanwhile, the cock sometimes mates with another female.

Location	Behaviour	Sketch
Date		
Time		
Weather	Field marks	
Call		

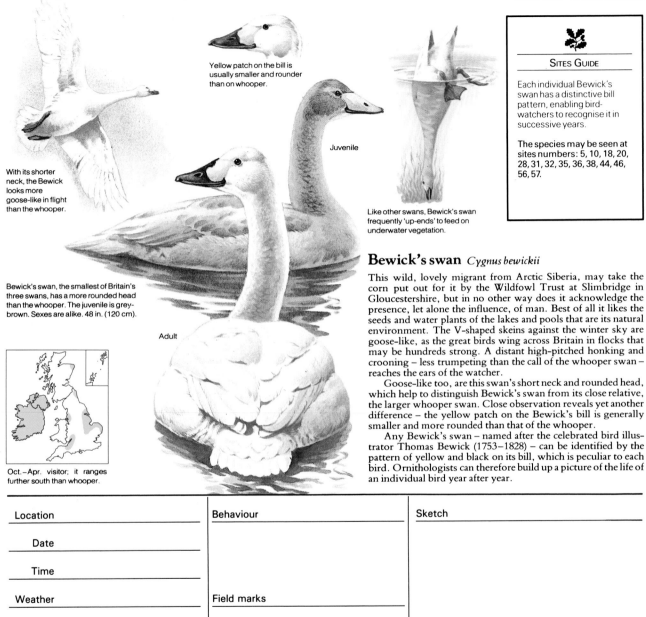

Yellow patch on the bill is usually smaller and rounder than on whooper.

Juvenile

With its shorter neck, the Bewick looks more goose-like in flight than the whooper.

Bewick's swan, the smallest of Britain's three swans, has a more rounded head than the whooper. The juvenile is grey-brown. Sexes are alike. 48 in. (120 cm).

Adult

Like other swans, Bewick's swan frequently 'up-ends' to feed on underwater vegetation.

Oct.–Apr. visitor; it ranges further south than whooper.

Bewick's swan *Cygnus bewickii*

This wild, lovely migrant from Arctic Siberia, may take the corn put out for it by the Wildfowl Trust at Slimbridge in Gloucestershire, but in no other way does it acknowledge the presence, let alone the influence, of man. Best of all it likes the seeds and water plants of the lakes and pools that are its natural environment. The V-shaped skeins against the winter sky are goose-like, as the great birds wing across Britain in flocks that may be hundreds strong. A distant high-pitched honking and crooning – less trumpeting than the call of the whooper swan – reaches the ears of the watcher.

Goose-like too, are this swan's short neck and rounded head, which help to distinguish Bewick's swan from its close relative, the larger whooper swan. Close observation reveals yet another difference – the yellow patch on the Bewick's bill is generally smaller and more rounded than that of the whooper.

Any Bewick's swan – named after the celebrated bird illustrator Thomas Bewick (1753–1828) – can be identified by the pattern of yellow and black on its bill, which is peculiar to each bird. Ornithologists can therefore build up a picture of the life of an individual bird year after year.

Location	Behaviour	Sketch
Date		
Time		
Weather	Field marks	
Call		

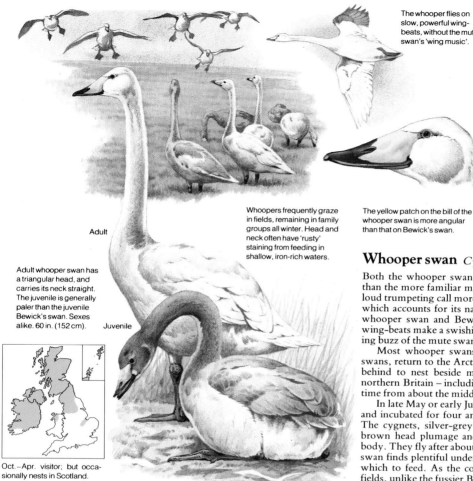

The whooper flies on slow, powerful wing-beats, without the mute swan's 'wing music'.

SITES GUIDE

The nest of the whooper swan is a mound of reeds and sedges with a depression in the top, sited on a snow-free bank near water.

The species may be seen at sites numbers: 5, 18, 28, 32, 41, 44, 45-47, 49, 50, 52, 53, 56, 57.

Adult

Whoopers frequently graze in fields, remaining in family groups all winter. Head and neck often have 'rusty' staining from feeding in shallow, iron-rich waters.

The yellow patch on the bill of the whooper swan is more angular than that on Bewick's swan.

Adult whooper swan has a triangular head, and carries its neck straight. The juvenile is generally paler than the juvenile Bewick's swan. Sexes alike. 60 in. (152 cm).

Juvenile

Oct.–Apr. visitor; but occasionally nests in Scotland.

Whooper swan *Cygnus cygnus*

Both the whooper swan and Bewick's swan are noisier birds than the more familiar mute swan; but the whooper swan has a loud trumpeting call more assertive than that of Bewick's swan, which accounts for its name. In flight, on the other hand, the whooper swan and Bewick's swan are relatively quiet: their wing-beats make a swishing sound, rather than the loud twanging buzz of the mute swan.

Most whooper swans, in company with all the Bewick's swans, return to the Arctic tundra to breed, but a few may stay behind to nest beside moorland tarns and desolate lochs in northern Britain – including Orkney, which they deserted for a time from about the middle of the 19th century.

In late May or early June a clutch of three to five eggs is laid, and incubated for four and a half to five weeks by the female. The cygnets, silver-grey and white at first, develop greyish-brown head plumage and white, grey-tipped feathers on the body. They fly after about eight weeks. In summer the whooper swan finds plentiful underwater plants, molluscs and insects on which to feed. As the cold closes in it will forage on stubble fields, unlike the fussier Bewick's swan.

Location	Behaviour	Sketch
Date		
Time		
Weather	Field marks	
Call		

Orange bill

Curved neck

Flight is powerful, with outstretched neck. When wings are beating, flight feathers produce loud, throbbing hum.

Curved neck which distinguishes adult mute swan is apparent even when swan rears out of water to repel an intruder. Male, or cob, has larger knob at base of orange bill than female. 60 in. (152 cm).

Cygnets (chicks) are pale grey above and white below; about six to a brood.

Threat display of adult male defending family consists of drawing back and folding wings above back while surging forward in water. Female often carries young on back.

Present all year; nests all over Britain except far north.

SITES GUIDE

Mute swans like still or sluggish waters with a supply of aquatic vegetation for food. Young birds are light brown.

The species may be seen at sites numbers: 1, 5, 7, 13, 16, 18, 21, 25, 27, 28, 36, 38, 40, 44, 48, 50, 53.

Mute swan *Cygnus olor*

This graceful bird's nature belies its placid, decorative appearance: it is extremely quarrelsome, and bullies smaller species. In the breeding season the male stakes out a large area of water and defends this territory aggressively against all-comers. The bird's name, too, is deceptive, for although quieter than Britain's two wild swans, the whooper and Bewick's, it hisses and snorts when angry, and may trumpet feebly.

All mute swans on the River Thames belong either to the Crown or to one of two London livery companies: the Vintners' Company and the Dyers' Company. In the third week of July, cygnets as far upstream as Henley-on-Thames are rounded up when they are flightless during the moult. Those that are owned by the livery companies are marked by having their bills notched; those left unmarked belong to the Crown. This 'swan-upping' ceremony dates back to the Middle Ages, when swans were highly valued as a table delicacy.

The nest is an enormous mound of water plants up to 13 ft (4 m) across and 30 in. (76 cm) high. Normally four to seven eggs are laid, and they are incubated for 34–38 days, mainly by the female, or pen. The young fly in four and a half months.

Location	Behaviour	Sketch
Date		
Time		
Weather	Field marks	
Call		

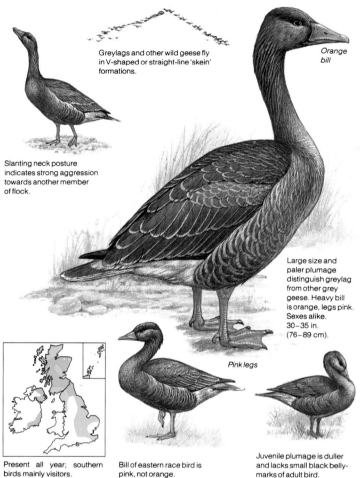

Greylags and other wild geese fly in V-shaped or straight-line 'skein' formations.

Orange bill

Slanting neck posture indicates strong aggression towards another member of flock.

Large size and paler plumage distinguish greylag from other grey geese. Heavy bill is orange, legs pink. Sexes alike. 30–35 in. (76–89 cm).

Pink legs

Present all year; southern birds mainly visitors.

Bill of eastern race bird is pink, not orange.

Juvenile plumage is duller and lacks small black belly-marks of adult bird.

Paired adults perform 'triumph ceremony' each time they meet.

SITES GUIDE

Greylag goslings take to water within hours of hatching. Nests are built of heather, grass or moss, on the ground near water.

The species may be seen at sites numbers: 37, 45-47, 49-51, 53, 58.

Greylag goose *Anser anser*

Greylags mate for life – and give their partners no chance to forget it. Every time they meet after any loss of contact, goose and gander go through a complicated ritual of posturing and calling that re-enacts their original courtship.

The greylag was once the only goose that bred in Britain, and may have earned its name by lagging behind when other species migrated. It was the ancestor of the familiar white farmyard goose, and its cackles and 'aang-ang-ang' honk in flight are similar to the sounds of the domestic bird. The greylag was once found as far south as the Fens, but was driven back to the remoter parts of Scotland when agricultural development destroyed its breeding grounds. In recent times, however, the bird has been re-introduced to many of its old areas, and new ones as far south as Kent.

Hilly Scottish heather moors, with a scattering of lochs, provide the greylag's most natural breeding ground. Unusually for a goose, it also inhabits sea islets. The descendants of re-introduced birds take readily to man-made freshwater sites. Goslings hatch after a month and fly after about two months, but stay in the family party until the following spring.

Location	Behaviour	Sketch
Date		
Time		
Weather	Field marks	
Call		

In flight, the darker forewing of the white-front distinguishes it from the pink-footed goose.

Adult bird has white forehead and black-barred underparts. Sexes are alike. 26–30 in. (66–76 cm).

White forehead

Flocks feed at night if moon is bright. They graze on pastures, plant shoots and grain.

Black bars

SITES GUIDE

White-fronted geese favour freshwater marshes and water-meadows during their winter stay in Britain.

The species may be seen at sites numbers: 20, 21, 28, 31, 32, 35, 45, 47, 60, 64.

Lesser white-fronted goose
Anser erythropus

This species, a rare visitor, is more slender, with a higher white face-patch and yellow eye-ring.

Oct.–Apr. visitor from Greenland and Siberia.

Bill of Greenland race is orange-yellow, not pink.

Immature bird's plumage shows fewer contrasts than adult's, and it lacks a white forehead. Orange legs and paler chest distinguish it from pink-footed goose.

White-fronted goose *Anser albifrons*

The white-fronted goose, or 'white front', is perhaps the most easily recognised of the grey geese, with its white forehead 'blaze' and its transverse black belly markings. White-fronts flock in from their Arctic breeding grounds in late September or early October. Those that come to western Scotland or Ireland are from Greenland, and have orange-yellow bills. Visitors to England breed in the far north of Russia; they have pinkish bills. Like greylags, mating white-fronts are paired for life, and reinforce their bond by repeating a similar courtship 'triumph ceremony' whenever they meet.

In flight, white-fronts may be distinguished by their call, which is higher pitched than that of other common geese. Even shriller in its call is the lesser white-fronted goose, which is classed as an 'accidental': flocks do not habitually migrate to Britain, but a few arrive among other species almost every year. It breeds in Arctic Scandinavia and Russia, and normally winters in the Balkans and south-west Asia.

The nest of both white-fronts is little more than a depression in the ground, lined with grass and down. Incubation takes up to four weeks, and the young fledge after five to six weeks.

Location	Behaviour	Sketch
Date		
Time		
Weather	Field marks	
Call		

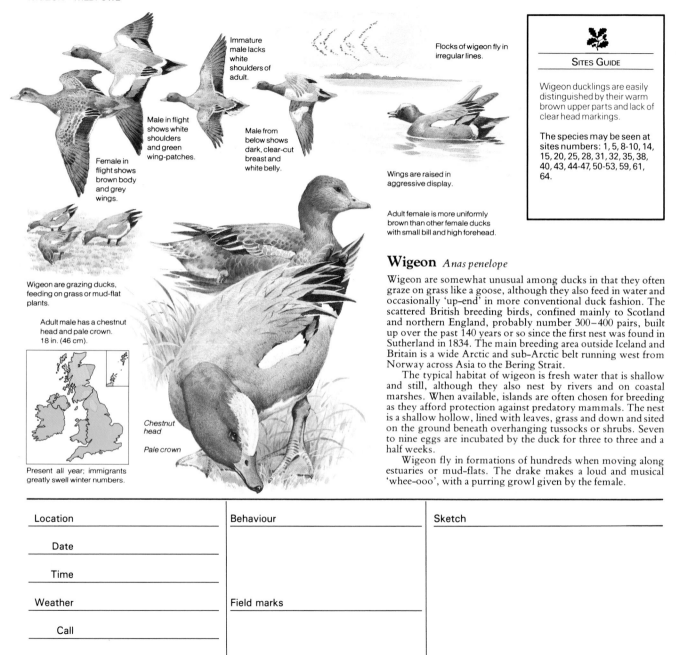

Immature male lacks white shoulders of adult.

Flocks of wigeon fly in irregular lines.

Male in flight shows white shoulders and green wing-patches.

Male from below shows dark, clear-cut breast and white belly.

Female in flight shows brown body and grey wings.

Wings are raised in aggressive display.

Wigeon are grazing ducks, feeding on grass or mud-flat plants.

Adult male has a chestnut head and pale crown. 18 in. (46 cm).

Chestnut head

Pale crown

Present all year; immigrants greatly swell winter numbers.

Adult female is more uniformly brown than other female ducks with small bill and high forehead.

SITES GUIDE

Wigeon ducklings are easily distinguished by their warm brown upper parts and lack of clear head markings.

The species may be seen at sites numbers: 1, 5, 8-10, 14, 15, 20, 25, 28, 31, 32, 35, 38, 40, 43, 44-47, 50-53, 59, 61, 64.

Wigeon *Anas penelope*

Wigeon are somewhat unusual among ducks in that they often graze on grass like a goose, although they also feed in water and occasionally 'up-end' in more conventional duck fashion. The scattered British breeding birds, confined mainly to Scotland and northern England, probably number 300–400 pairs, built up over the past 140 years or so since the first nest was found in Sutherland in 1834. The main breeding area outside Iceland and Britain is a wide Arctic and sub-Arctic belt running west from Norway across Asia to the Bering Strait.

The typical habitat of wigeon is fresh water that is shallow and still, although they also nest by rivers and on coastal marshes. When available, islands are often chosen for breeding as they afford protection against predatory mammals. The nest is a shallow hollow, lined with leaves, grass and down and sited on the ground beneath overhanging tussocks or shrubs. Seven to nine eggs are incubated by the duck for three to three and a half weeks.

Wigeon fly in formations of hundreds when moving along estuaries or mud-flats. The drake makes a loud and musical 'whee-ooo', with a purring growl given by the female.

Location	Behaviour	Sketch
Date		
Time		
Weather	Field marks	
Call		

Black head, neck

White chin-patch

Aggressive displays include a threat posture with head lowered nearly to ground level.

Flightless like most wildfowl during the post-breeding moult, birds move first to safe waters.

Long neck and deep wing-beats are distinctive in flight.

Present all year; introduced species.

Head and neck have unmistakable pattern. Sexes are alike. 36–40 in. (90–100 cm).

Juvenile bird has duller chin-patch and more mottled upper parts than adult; but first winter plumage resembles that of adult.

SITES GUIDE

The nest of the Canada goose is a ground hollow lined with leaves, grass and down. The gander often stands guard beside his mate.

The species may be seen at sites numbers: 18, 21, 25, 27, 37, 38.

Canada goose *Branta canadensis*

Extreme tameness has saved the Canada goose from becoming a popular target for wildfowlers and probably helped to give it the chance to establish itself as a wild breeding bird in Britain. The first Canada geese were brought across the Atlantic in the 17th century as decorative birds for parkland lakes. Attempts were later made to develop their numbers for shooting, but the bird is too tame, too irregular in its flighting times and flies too low to make it a 'sporting target'. It has now spread out of its parkland homes, and a countrywide census in 1976 revealed a population of more than 19,000 birds.

Although a large bird, the Canada goose can be unobtrusive when resting or feeding. Suddenly, however, a party may start calling with a trumpet-like honking. The noise builds up and the geese take wing, continuing their calls as they make for a neighbouring stretch of water.

The nest of the Canada goose consists of plant material at the water's edge or on an island. The female lays five or six creamy–white eggs in April or May. From these are hatched greenish-yellow or brown goslings. They can fly after nine weeks, but remain as a family until the following spring.

Location	Behaviour	Sketch
Date		
Time		
Weather	Field marks	
Call		

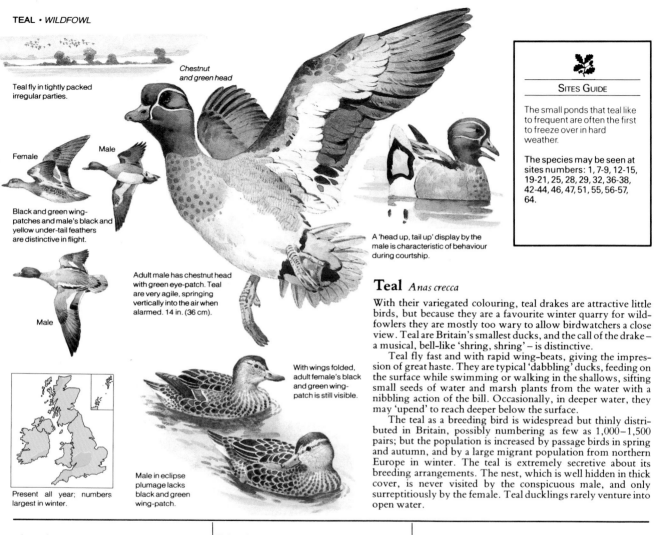

Teal fly in tightly packed irregular parties.

Chestnut and green head

Female

Male

Black and green wing-patches and male's black and yellow under-tail feathers are distinctive in flight.

Male

Adult male has chestnut head with green eye-patch. Teal are very agile, springing vertically into the air when alarmed. 14 in. (36 cm).

With wings folded, adult female's black and green wing-patch is still visible.

A 'head up, tail up' display by the male is characteristic of behaviour during courtship.

Present all year; numbers largest in winter.

Male in eclipse plumage lacks black and green wing-patch.

SITES GUIDE

The small ponds that teal like to frequent are often the first to freeze over in hard weather.

The species may be seen at sites numbers: 1, 7-9, 12-15, 19-21, 25, 28, 29, 32, 36-38, 42-44, 46, 47, 51, 55, 56-57, 64.

Teal *Anas crecca*

With their variegated colouring, teal drakes are attractive little birds, but because they are a favourite winter quarry for wild-fowlers they are mostly too wary to allow birdwatchers a close view. Teal are Britain's smallest ducks, and the call of the drake – a musical, bell-like 'shring, shring' – is distinctive.

Teal fly fast and with rapid wing-beats, giving the impression of great haste. They are typical 'dabbling' ducks, feeding on the surface while swimming or walking in the shallows, sifting small seeds of water and marsh plants from the water with a nibbling action of the bill. Occasionally, in deeper water, they may 'upend' to reach deeper below the surface.

The teal as a breeding bird is widespread but thinly distributed in Britain, possibly numbering as few as 1,000–1,500 pairs; but the population is increased by passage birds in spring and autumn, and by a large migrant population from northern Europe in winter. The teal is extremely secretive about its breeding arrangements. The nest, which is well hidden in thick cover, is never visited by the conspicuous male, and only surreptitiously by the female. Teal ducklings rarely venture into open water.

Location	Behaviour	Sketch
Date		
Time		
Weather	Field marks	
Call		

Female

Male

Sharp-pointed wings and wing-patches are conspicuous in flight.

Swimming posture is high, with wing and tail raised.

Male

Gadwalls 'up-end' often, like all dabbling ducks.

Male courtship display emphasises wing and tail colour contrasts.

Wing-patches distinguish female gadwall from female mallard.

Black coverts

Present all year, but rather thinly distributed.

Adult male's most prominent features are black tail coverts and red-brown, black and white wing-patches. 20 in. (50 cm).

SITES GUIDE

The gadwall duckling is like a young mallard, but with more contrast in colouring, bigger back-patches and pinkish bill-sides.

The species may be seen at sites numbers: 1, 2, 7, 10, 15, 16, 21, 32, 34, 38, 40, 41, 43, 45, 50, 51, 61.

Gadwall *Anas strepera*

Language experts offer no clue as to how the gadwall got its name, which centuries ago was written as 'gadwell' or 'gaddel'. But before 1850, when a visiting pair were trapped and wing-clipped, this duck was known only as a winter immigrant. Today a few breed in Scotland and winter mainly in Ireland, but most of the 100–200 pairs that breed in Britain are concentrated in East Anglia, where they are descended from captive stock.

The drake of this species, whose true homelands are central and western Asia and western North America, is rather drab. The bird's voice is unremarkable too: various grunts and whistles from the male and a mallard-like quack from the female.

Eggs are laid at the end of April in a ground hollow, lined with grass or leaves, insulated with down pulled from the duck's breast and well hidden in thick vegetation. They are covered if unattended during the month-long incubation period, and the hatched ducklings are shepherded out of the nest as soon as their down dries. Easy prey for predators, they stand a better chance by keeping on the move. Gadwalls are vegetarian for all but the first week of life, when the ducklings feed themselves on protein-rich insects, snails and worms.

Location	Behaviour	Sketch
Date		
Time		
Weather	Field marks	
Call		

Male mallards are often seen in pursuit of a female in flight.

In communal courtship displays, males pull their necks well back and often flick water with their bills.

When moulting, July–Sept., the flight-less male resembles female, except for yellow bill.

Pairs often nest high in a waterside tree. Newly hatched ducklings have to drop to the ground.

Green head

Maroon breast

The adult female has a greenish-yellow bill and violet-blue wing-patch.

Present all year; many from west Europe winter in Britain.

Adult male has glossy green head, white collar, maroon breast and curly black tail-feathers. The mallard is the biggest of the surface-feeding ducks in the British Isles. 23 in. (58 cm).

Mallard *Anas platyrhynchos*

In both town and country, the mallard is the most familiar duck in the British Isles. It is as much at home on a park lake or city canal as it is on a quiet country backwater or remote reservoir. Mallards living near towns have learned to live side by side with man, often relying on him to supplement their diet with bread and other scraps of food. Country-dwelling birds, however, have learned to fear humans, because of the activities of wild-fowlers.

The mallard is typical of the 'dabbling' ducks in that it feeds on the surface of the water and can spring straight up into the air with a powerful whirring of wings. Its broad, flattened bill is adapted for filtering from the water a wide range of tiny plant and animal matter. The webbed, paddle-like feet are placed well back on the mallard's body so that it walks with a rolling waddle from side to side.

The female mallard makes the quacking sound that people associate with ducks. The drake, however, also gives an occasional subdued, hoarse-sounding 'raarb' call, especially when suspicious or alarmed. Nests are made from leaves and grass, and lined with down. They are generally well-concealed.

Location	Behaviour	Sketch
Date		
Time		
Weather	Field marks	
Call		

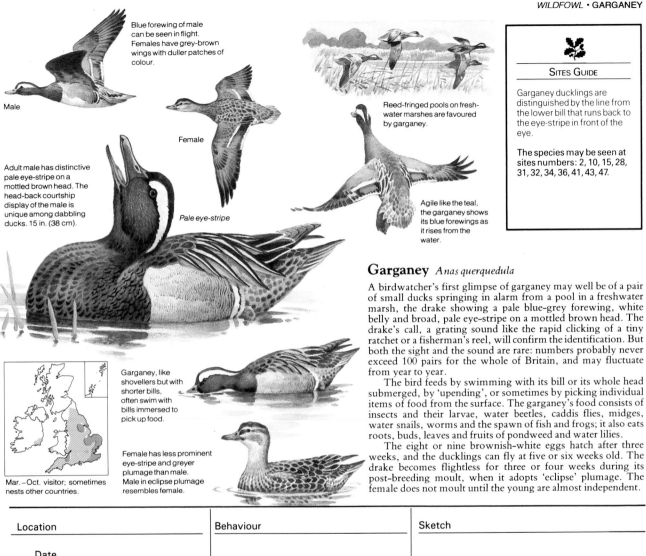

Blue forewing of male can be seen in flight. Females have grey-brown wings with duller patches of colour.

Male

Female

Adult male has distinctive pale eye-stripe on a mottled brown head. The head-back courtship display of the male is unique among dabbling ducks. 15 in. (38 cm).

Pale eye-stripe

Reed-fringed pools on fresh-water marshes are favoured by garganey.

Agile like the teal, the garganey shows its blue forewings as it rises from the water.

SITES GUIDE

Garganey ducklings are distinguished by the line from the lower bill that runs back to the eye-stripe in front of the eye.

The species may be seen at sites numbers: 2, 10, 15, 28, 31, 32, 34, 36, 41, 43, 47.

Garganey, like shovellers but with shorter bills, often swim with bills immersed to pick up food.

Mar.–Oct. visitor; sometimes nests other countries.

Female has less prominent eye-stripe and greyer plumage than male. Male in eclipse plumage resembles female.

Garganey *Anas querquedula*

A birdwatcher's first glimpse of garganey may well be of a pair of small ducks springing in alarm from a pool in a freshwater marsh, the drake showing a pale blue-grey forewing, white belly and broad, pale eye-stripe on a mottled brown head. The drake's call, a grating sound like the rapid clicking of a tiny ratchet or a fisherman's reel, will confirm the identification. But both the sight and the sound are rare: numbers probably never exceed 100 pairs for the whole of Britain, and may fluctuate from year to year.

The bird feeds by swimming with its bill or its whole head submerged, by 'upending', or sometimes by picking individual items of food from the surface. The garganey's food consists of insects and their larvae, water beetles, caddis flies, midges, water snails, worms and the spawn of fish and frogs; it also eats roots, buds, leaves and fruits of pondweed and water lilies.

The eight or nine brownish-white eggs hatch after three weeks, and the ducklings can fly at five or six weeks old. The drake becomes flightless for three or four weeks during its post-breeding moult, when it adopts 'eclipse' plumage. The female does not moult until the young are almost independent.

Location	Behaviour	Sketch
Date		
Time		
Weather	Field marks	
Call		

27

Male in flight. Both sexes in flight show blue shoulder, white bar and green rear patch on wing.

Green head

Male in 'eclipse' plumage, during flightless stage of moulting, has brighter wings than female but darker back.

Shovel bill

White breast

Adult male has glossy green head like that of mallard, but breast is white and belly chestnut. Huge 'shovel' bill is unmistakable in both sexes. 20 in. (50 cm).

Present all year; joined by winter migrants.

Adult female has brown head and body with speckled underparts. Specialised bill development soon starts to show in ducklings.

Shoveler *Anas clypeata*

The most distinctive feature of the shoveler is the long, rounded, spade–like bill that gives the bird its name. The bill is used in the typical manner of dabbling ducks for sifting large volumes of water to filter out particles of food. This includes buds and seeds of water plants such as reeds and sedges, as well as algae and small molluscs. Crustaceans and insects are eaten, and so are tadpoles and spawn. The inside edges of the bill have numerous comb–like 'teeth' to trap food as water is forced through them.

The shoveler is a handsome but uncommon bird, with a very patchy distribution governed partly by the availability of its habitat – marshy areas with pools, ditches and other areas of open water that have muddy shallows rich in food. The nest, like that of most of the shoveler's close relatives, is a shallow hollow in the ground lined with grass, feathers and down.

There may be between seven and 14 pale greenish eggs in a clutch, laid from April onwards. The female incubates them for about three and a half weeks. The ducklings, which are led away from the nest as soon as all have hatched and dried, soon show signs of developing outsize bills, and can fly when about six to seven weeks old. Only one brood is reared each year.

Location	Behaviour	Sketch
Date		
Time		
Weather	Field marks	
Call		

Chocolate head

Male

Female

The long slender neck, pointed wings and light rear wing edge are conspicuous in flight. Wings have a black and bronze patch.

Flocks of pintails are often seen flying in an uneven 'V' formation.

Long tail

Adult female is pale brown and, like the male, slim and rakish in build.

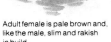

Present all year; rare as breeding bird.

In moult, drake resembles female, but upper parts more uniform in colour.

Adult male has chocolate and white head pattern and a long pointed tail. The tail feathers can add an extra 8 in. (20 cm) to the bird's body length of 22 in. (55 cm).

Communal courtship displays by males include a head-stretching posture, with a burping call.

Pintail *Anas acuta*

Both on the ground and in the air, this is the most elegant of the British ducks. Its long slender neck, wings and tail, combined with its subtle colouring, make it easy to recognise and attractive to watch. A flock passing high overhead makes a beautiful picture. The watcher can also hear the drakes' faint wheezing 'geeeee' calls and the ducks' rattling sounds.

Most pintails spend only the winter in Britain. None was known to breed in the British Isles before 1869, and even now the breeding population probably rarely reaches 50 pairs. They rarely nest on the same site for more than a couple of years, so it is difficult to make an accurate count, even though the nest is often less camouflaged than that of other ducks.

Breeding begins in mid-April in southern Britain, but not until two months later in the north. Usually there are seven or eight eggs, varying in colour from creamy-yellow to pale green or blue. As is usual in waterfowl, the duck incubates the eggs, camouflaged by her dull colouring, and defends the nest and the ducklings with distraction displays. The ducklings – brown with white stripes and greyish-white underparts – take to the water as soon as they are hatched; they fly after seven weeks.

Location	Behaviour	Sketch
Date		
Time		
Weather	Field marks	
Call		

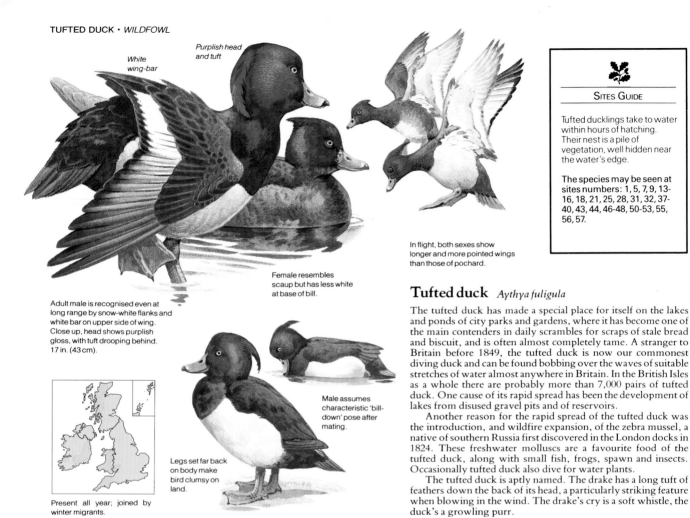

White wing-bar

Purplish head and tuft

Adult male is recognised even at long range by snow-white flanks and white bar on upper side of wing. Close up, head shows purplish gloss, with tuft drooping behind. 17 in. (43 cm).

Female resembles scaup but has less white at base of bill.

In flight, both sexes show longer and more pointed wings than those of pochard.

Male assumes characteristic 'bill-down' pose after mating.

Legs set far back on body make bird clumsy on land.

Present all year; joined by winter migrants.

SITES GUIDE

Tufted ducklings take to water within hours of hatching. Their nest is a pile of vegetation, well hidden near the water's edge.

The species may be seen at sites numbers: 1, 5, 7, 9, 13-16, 18, 21, 25, 28, 31, 32, 37-40, 43, 44, 46-48, 50-53, 55, 56, 57.

Tufted duck *Aythya fuligula*

The tufted duck has made a special place for itself on the lakes and ponds of city parks and gardens, where it has become one of the main contenders in daily scrambles for scraps of stale bread and biscuit, and is often almost completely tame. A stranger to Britain before 1849, the tufted duck is now our commonest diving duck and can be found bobbing over the waves of suitable stretches of water almost anywhere in Britain. In the British Isles as a whole there are probably more than 7,000 pairs of tufted duck. One cause of its rapid spread has been the development of lakes from disused gravel pits and of reservoirs.

Another reason for the rapid spread of the tufted duck was the introduction, and wildfire expansion, of the zebra mussel, a native of southern Russia first discovered in the London docks in 1824. These freshwater molluscs are a favourite food of the tufted duck, along with small fish, frogs, spawn and insects. Occasionally tufted duck also dive for water plants.

The tufted duck is aptly named. The drake has a long tuft of feathers down the back of its head, a particularly striking feature when blowing in the wind. The drake's cry is a soft whistle, the duck's a growling purr.

Location	Behaviour	Sketch
Date		
Time		
Weather	Field marks	
Call		

Red head

Grey back

Black breast

In courtship, the male bird may jerk head onto back while emitting a soft, wheezing whistle.

Adult female is dull brown, with pale face markings and light streaks on back and flanks.

Feeding dive starts with a small jump.

Take-off is laborious, with a pattering run across the water. Once launched, the bird's flight is fast.

Present all year; joined by winter migrants.

Adult male's brick-red head, black breast and grey back are distinctive. Both sexes have grey wing-bars. 18 in. (45 cm).

Pochard *Aythya ferina*

Like its close relative the tufted duck, the pochard habitually nests in reed-beds and other vegetation around inland stretches of fresh water. Unlike the tufted duck, however, the pochard has not yet bred to any great extent on the vast acreage of wetland created in recent years by man – sand pits, gravel pits and reservoirs.

The pochard chooses its nesting site carefully, requiring an area of open water free from floating plants but rich in the submerged vegetation that provides food – seeds, leaves, tubers, crustaceans, molluscs, worms and insects. This food the pochard gathers by diving down to about 3–8 ft (1–2·5 m). The pochard particularly favours lakes with tall vegetation fringing them, and sheltered islands with cover, in which the nest will be safe from most mammal predators.

The nest is either a shallow cup in the ground, lined with reeds and leaves, or a platform with a cup built up from the bottom in shallow water. In either case, it is lined with down. The eggs are greenish-grey, and a typical clutch numbers from 6–12 eggs. The pochard is rather a silent species: the most frequent call is a harsh, purring 'kerrr' uttered by the female.

Location	Behaviour	Sketch
Date		
Time		
Weather	Field marks	
Call		

Male

Female

Flight is fast and direct, with neck and body outstretched to produce a long, narrow shape. White wing-patch is more extensive on male.

Double crest

Red-brown breast

Fishing birds often swim with head under water before submerging totally to dive on prey.

During its moult the male resembles the female, but back is darker and forewing whiter.

Adult female in breeding plumage has shorter crest than the male. The brown colouring of the head merges into neck and breast.

Present all year; mainly on estuaries in winter.

Downy young are generally dark above and pale below, with white spots on their wings and backs.

Adult male has dark green head and reddish-brown breast and neck. Double crest and darker colouring distinguish it from goosander. 23 in. (58 cm).

Sites Guide

The female red-breasted merganser alone tends the ducklings. Nests are built near rivers or lakes and only one brood is reared each year.

The species may be seen at sites numbers: 28, 32, 37, 44, 47, 52, 56, 57.

Red-breasted merganser *Mergus serrator*

These ducks have a bad reputation among trout and salmon fishermen because of their taste for the young of the two fish. Defenders of the red-breasted merganser argue, however, that they also eat many non-game species, including eels, perch and pike which compete with or prey on the eggs or the young of salmon and trout.

The red-breasted merganser and the goosander are the only two species of sawbill duck that breed in the British Isles. They have finely serrated cutting edges to their bills that enable them to grasp slippery fish. The red-breasted merganser has a long history of residence in Scotland and Ireland. Since about 1950, however, in spite of some persecution, birds have spread into England, breeding as far south as Derbyshire, and also into Wales.

The nest is a shallow depression in the ground lined with grass, leaves and down. Thick vegetation usually makes it hard to find. From late April to early July the female lays and incubates eight to ten pale buff eggs that take a month to hatch. When the female leaves the nest, she camouflages the eggs with down. The ducklings can fly about two months after hatching.

Location	Behaviour	Sketch
Date		
Time		
Weather	Field marks	
Call		

Hollow trees are favourite nesting places.

Bill-raising and water-splashing are courtship gestures. The 'threat crouch' is a characteristic aggressive display.

On the water the male appears mainly white, its black head showing a green sheen. It has a white spot on each cheek.

Female has brown and white plumage.

Wing-patches

High forehead, short bill

Mainly Sept.–Apr. visitor, but now nests in Scotland.

Adult male has black and white plumage. Both sexes are distinguished in flight by rectangular white wing-patches, high foreheads and short bills. 18 in. (45 cm).

SITES GUIDE

Goldeneye form large winter flocks, in most cases of one sex. They stay mostly on the water, rarely coming ashore.

The species may be seen at sites numbers: 1, 7, 8, 10, 13, 14, 25, 28, 31, 35, 37–41, 43–50, 52, 53, 56, 57.

Goldeneye *Bucephala clangula*

In 1970 a goldeneye duck and four large ducklings were spotted swimming on a small loch in central Scotland. This was the first proof that the goldeneye had bred successfully in the British Isles. Normally the goldeneye is a winter visitor that breeds in northern Scandinavia and northern Asia. It prefers to nest in tree-holes near a lake or a river, but also uses rabbit burrows and specially provided nest-boxes. On the Continent, goldeneye have often taken over the old nest holes of black woodpeckers.

The bottom of the goldeneye's nesting cavity is unlined, but simply insulated with some greyish-white down and a few feathers. A typical clutch numbers 6–12 smooth, greenish-blue eggs. The young scramble out of the hole and fall to the ground, often a considerable drop; they generally survive unharmed, and those that do take about eight weeks fully to develop their flight feathers.

Goldeneye in flight have the fast wing-beats typical of diving ducks, but they take off more easily than most, and the wings produce a pronounced whistling sound which is quite unmistakable. In winter many goldeneye take to coastal waters, but some small flocks may be found on larger stretches of inland water.

Location	Behaviour	Sketch
Date		
Time		
Weather	Field marks	
Call		

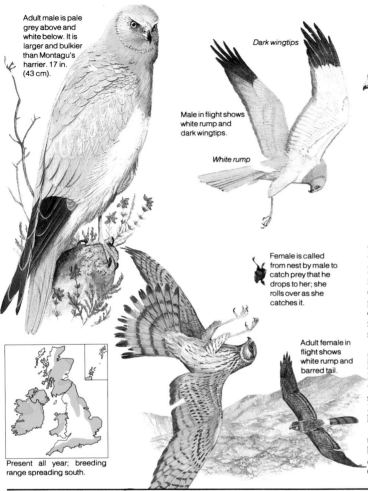

Adult male is pale grey above and white below. It is larger and bulkier than Montagu's harrier. 17 in. (43 cm).

Dark wingtips

Male in flight shows white rump and dark wingtips.

White rump

Female is called from nest by male to catch prey that he drops to her; she rolls over as she catches it.

Adult female in flight shows white rump and barred tail.

Adult female is brown above and brown-and-white streaked below, with black bars on its wings. It is larger than the male. 20 in. (50 cm).

Present all year; breeding range spreading south.

Hen harrier *Circus cyaneus*

Pouncing from a low-level hunting glide, this moorland marauder is far from particular about its prey. Almost any creature up to the size of a hare or a duck is fair game for its powerful talons. Small mammals and birds, including the chicks of other birds of prey, make up most of the hen harrier's diet, but it also eats lizards, snakes, frogs, beetles and the eggs of ground-nesting birds.

Centuries ago, when the bird was more widespread, it preyed on domestic poultry and so obtained its name; today, however, it is considered to be little threat to the farmyard hen. Hen harriers became very rare in the early part of this century, vanishing entirely from mainland Britain by about 1940 and surviving only in the Orkneys and Outer Hebrides. Since all Britain's hawks gained the protection of the law, however, hen harriers have shown a particularly large population increase.

Breeding areas of the hen harrier are now spreading back through England, Wales and Ireland, and birds are nesting in birch and willow scrub, young fir plantations and even among crops, as well as in their traditional moor and marsh areas. Chicks hatch in about five weeks and fly at five weeks old.

Location	Behaviour	Sketch
Date		
Time		
Weather	Field marks	
Call		

The female is the biggest of all harriers, dark brown with a pale crown, throat and forewing. 23 in. (58 cm).

Young are coloured like the female but have no yellow on the forewing.

The older male has pale colouring under the wings. The head is also pale and the underparts are reddish-streaked. 20 in. (50 cm).

Pale head

Reddish underparts

Present all year; the young move south in winter.

Pale shoulders of female are distinctive. In the marsh harrier's flight, slow, steady flaps alternate with glides.

The male is unique among harriers in having a dark back, grey tail and pale head.

Wings are held in a shallow V when gliding or soaring.

SITES GUIDE

The marsh harrier builds a substantial nest of reeds among marsh plants. The young may leave it before they are fully fledged.

The species may be seen at sites numbers: 34-37, 47, 52, 53.

Marsh harrier *Circus aeruginosus*

Once quite common, this powerful hawk is today one of Britain's rarest birds. Increasing use of pesticides, drainage of the fens and, not least, persecution by man probably contributed to the bird's decline. Recently, however, there has been a slight increase in numbers. There are now about 18 pairs in Britain – but they rarely succeed in raising young.

The female is larger than the male and is almost as big as a buzzard, though not so heavily built. Both male and female birds, in common with other harriers, have face feathers arranged to give them an owl-like appearance. This probably serves to funnel sound into the ears – a great advantage to a bird that hunts its prey in dense reeds or grass.

In Britain, marsh harriers generally remain near the breeding grounds all winter. At the approach of spring, the pairs begin their display ritual. They fly up to a height of several thousand feet before diving and somersaulting downwards, swooping upwards again near the ground. The male often passes food to the female during these displays, and this must help to nourish her in preparation for egg-laying. Four to five bluish-white eggs make up the average clutch.

Location	Behaviour	Sketch
Date		
Time		
Weather	Field marks	
Call		

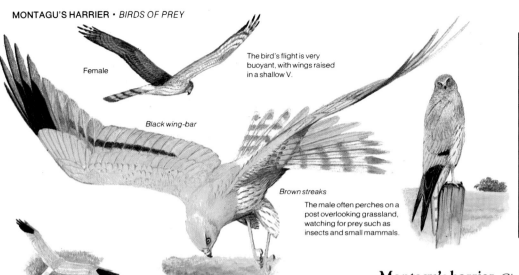

Female

The bird's flight is very buoyant, with wings raised in a shallow V.

Black wing-bar

Brown streaks

The male often perches on a post overlooking grassland, watching for prey such as insects and small mammals.

SITES GUIDE

An uncommon visitor, the Montagu's harrier nests on the ground among vegetation in open country, from farmland to sand dunes.

The species may be seen at sites numbers: 33, 34.

Pallid harrier
Circus macrourus

This harrier is a vagrant, slimmer than Montagu's harrier and even rarer. The male is very pale in colour.

Late Apr.–Sept. visitor; only one or two pairs breed.

Adult male is slighter-built than the hen harrier, with black wing-bar and brown streaks on whitish under-wing and flanks. 16 in. (40 cm).

Immature bird resembles female, but has unstreaked, chestnut underparts.

Adult female is generally similar to the hen harrier but slightly smaller, with a narrower white rump-patch. 18 in. (45 cm).

Montagu's harrier *Circus pygargus*

A Montagu's harrier is so easy to confuse with a hen harrier that it was not until 1802 that George Montagu, the Devon naturalist who compiled an early dictionary of birds, distinguished between them and gave one his name. Only the immature birds, with their chestnut underparts, are distinctive. The two birds differ also in their breeding habits. The hen harrier is a well-established breeding bird in the north and west, while the Montagu's harrier is one of Britain's rarest breeding birds, limited to a few pairs in southern England.

Migrants arrive from the Mediterranean and tropical Africa in April and settle down in their pairs by the end of May or early June. The eggs are laid at intervals of up to two or three days, and since the female starts to incubate after laying the first egg, the young hatch at similar intervals after four weeks.

The female greets the male as he brings food for her and the chicks. In common with most harriers, the prey is passed from foot to foot in mid-air, or dropped by the male and caught by the female. After about three weeks, the female shares in the hunting to satisfy the appetites of the growing family, which take wing after about five weeks.

Location	Behaviour	Sketch
Date		
Time		
Weather	Field marks	
Call		

Perching buzzard has an upright stance and shows a heavy, rounded build.

In gliding, wings are held flat with primary feathers turned back and pointed.

Wings are held forward and raised when soaring, with primary feathers turned up and tail widely spread.

Legs are unfeathered, unlike those of the visiting rough-legged buzzard.

Short neck

Finely barred tail

Adult in its most frequent colouring. Buzzards range in colour from dark grey or brown to the palest grey. Sexes are alike. 20–22 in. (50–55 cm).

Present all year; rare outside breeding range.

Buzzard *Buteo buteo*

A familiar sound in hilly country in western or northern Britain is the mewing 'kiew' of a buzzard as it sails apparently without effort over a neighbouring hillside, circling in the updraught from the hill or in a rising thermal of hot air. The keen-sighted bird meanwhile scans the ground below for prey. Small mammals are its favourite food, in particular rabbits – so much so that the number of buzzards declined dramatically after myxomatosis almost wiped out Britain's rabbit population in the mid-1950s.

Buzzards prefer open hillsides and wooded valleys like those of South Wales, the Lake District and western Scotland; they are fewer in bare, mountainous regions and moorland. They build large nests of sticks or heather stalks and line them with finer twigs, bracken, grass, moss or seaweed.

The handsome eggs have a white or bluish-white shell decorated with brown spots or blotches. They take about a month to hatch, and since the eggs are laid at intervals of three or four days the young are of variable age. Young birds often die of starvation when food is short, but despite this, buzzards remain the most common of Britain's larger birds of prey.

Location	Behaviour	Sketch
Date		
Time		
Weather	Field marks	
Call		

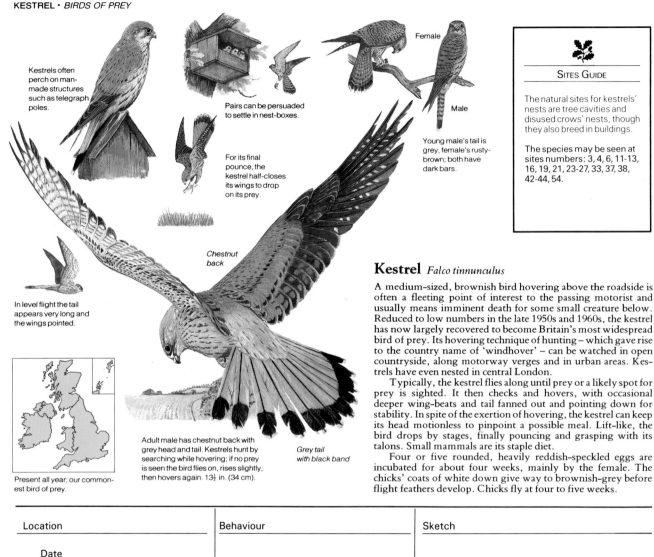

Kestrels often perch on man-made structures such as telegraph poles.

Pairs can be persuaded to settle in nest-boxes.

For its final pounce, the kestrel half-closes its wings to drop on its prey.

Female

Male

Young male's tail is grey, female's rusty-brown; both have dark bars.

Chestnut back

In level flight the tail appears very long and the wings pointed.

Adult male has chestnut back with grey head and tail. Kestrels hunt by searching while hovering; if no prey is seen the bird flies on, rises slightly, then hovers again. 13½ in. (34 cm).

Grey tail with black band

Present all year; our commonest bird of prey.

Kestrel *Falco tinnunculus*

A medium-sized, brownish bird hovering above the roadside is often a fleeting point of interest to the passing motorist and usually means imminent death for some small creature below. Reduced to low numbers in the late 1950s and 1960s, the kestrel has now largely recovered to become Britain's most widespread bird of prey. Its hovering technique of hunting – which gave rise to the country name of 'windhover' – can be watched in open countryside, along motorway verges and in urban areas. Kestrels have even nested in central London.

Typically, the kestrel flies along until prey or a likely spot for prey is sighted. It then checks and hovers, with occasional deeper wing-beats and tail fanned out and pointing down for stability. In spite of the exertion of hovering, the kestrel can keep its head motionless to pinpoint a possible meal. Lift-like, the bird drops by stages, finally pouncing and grasping with its talons. Small mammals are its staple diet.

Four or five rounded, heavily reddish-speckled eggs are incubated for about four weeks, mainly by the female. The chicks' coats of white down give way to brownish-grey before flight feathers develop. Chicks fly at four to five weeks.

Location	Behaviour	Sketch
Date		
Time		
Weather	Field marks	
Call		

Orange-brown face

In flight, the partridge's red-brown tail is noticeable.

Horseshoe mark

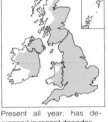

Coveys of birds disturbed while feeding keep together even in flight.

Adult male has distinctive dark brown horseshoe mark on lower breast. It has a grey neck and breast, and an orange-brown face. 12 in. (30 cm).

SITES GUIDE

A partridge incubates its eggs in a hollow scrape in the ground, blending so well with its surroundings as to be almost invisible.

The species may be seen at sites numbers: 6, 13, 14, 16, 19, 22, 23, 25-27, 29, 33, 36, 37, 39, 42, 44.

Present all year; has decreased in recent decades.

Female's markings are duller than those of male, and lack clear mark on underparts. Chicks are marked with clear bands.

Partridge *Perdix perdix*

The partridge is one of the most popular game birds, and Britain's partridge population has frequently been boosted by imports from the Continent, particularly from eastern Europe: hence its alternative name of Hungarian partridge. It is also known as the common or grey partridge, to distinguish it from the French, or red-legged, partridge. Shooting starts early in September, when the birds are gathered together in family flocks, or coveys.

By February the surviving birds have paired off and the cock birds spiritedly defend their territory against rivals. Courtship often takes the form of a running chase, the cock and hen taking it in turns to pursue each other. The nest is a hollow scrape in the ground in suitable cover such as under a hedge, growing corn or tall grass. From 10 to 20 eggs are laid, olive-brown in colour, but partridges are prolific layers and two or more birds will often lay eggs in one nest, so that clutches of up to 40 may occur.

The partridge's call is a grating 'karr-wick', repeated at intervals. When startled they leap into the air with an explosive 'krikrikrik . . .', repeated rapidly at first but slowing down as the birds escape from danger.

Location	Behaviour	Sketch
Date		
Time		
Weather	Field marks	
Call		

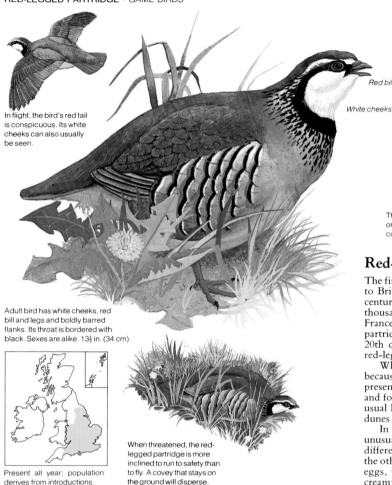

In flight, the bird's red tail is conspicuous. Its white cheeks can also usually be seen.

Red bill

White cheeks

The bird is fond of perching on a fence post or other convenient object.

Adult bird has white cheeks, red bill and legs and boldly barred flanks. Its throat is bordered with black. Sexes are alike. 13½ in. (34 cm).

Present all year; population derives from introductions.

When threatened, the red-legged partridge is more inclined to run to safety than to fly. A covey that stays on the ground will disperse.

SITES GUIDE

The nest of the red-legged partridge is sparsely lined with dried grass. It is usually in long grass or under brambles.

The species may be seen at sites numbers: 1, 23, 27, 29, 30, 33, 37, 42.

Red-legged partridge *Alectoris rufa*

The first recorded attempt to introduce the red-legged partridge to Britain took place in 1673; but it was not until more than a century later that the species really became established. In 1790 thousands of chicks were reared from eggs imported from France, and the bird is still sometimes known as the French partridge. Scores of further imports occurred in the 19th and 20th centuries, and today – particularly in East Anglia – the red-leg outnumbers the native species.

When flushed, the bird often runs rather than flies, and because of this, some sportsmen complain that it does not present a good target for their guns. It tends to remain in cover, and for such a colourful bird, it blends remarkably well with its usual habitats, such as ploughed fields, heaths, downs, coastal dunes and open countryside.

In the breeding season, the red-legged partridge has the unusual habit of sometimes laying two clutches of eggs in different nests. One of these is incubated by the female bird, and the other by the male. Each clutch may consist of 10–20 or more eggs, which are laid at 36 hour intervals. The eggs are a pale, creamy-brown with a few reddish-brown speckles.

Location	Behaviour	Sketch
Date		
Time		
Weather	Field marks	
Call		

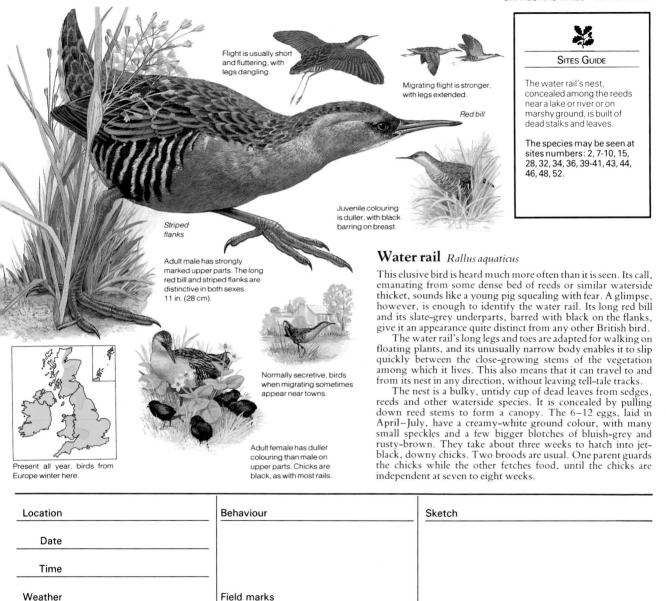

Flight is usually short and fluttering, with legs dangling.

Migrating flight is stronger, with legs extended.

Red bill

Juvenile colouring is duller, with black barring on breast.

Striped flanks

Adult male has strongly marked upper parts. The long red bill and striped flanks are distinctive in both sexes. 11 in. (28 cm).

Normally secretive, birds when migrating sometimes appear near towns.

Adult female has duller colouring than male on upper parts. Chicks are black, as with most rails.

Present all year, birds from Europe winter here.

Water rail *Rallus aquaticus*

This elusive bird is heard much more often than it is seen. Its call, emanating from some dense bed of reeds or similar waterside thicket, sounds like a young pig squealing with fear. A glimpse, however, is enough to identify the water rail. Its long red bill and its slate-grey underparts, barred with black on the flanks, give it an appearance quite distinct from any other British bird.

The water rail's long legs and toes are adapted for walking on floating plants, and its unusually narrow body enables it to slip quickly between the close-growing stems of the vegetation among which it lives. This also means that it can travel to and from its nest in any direction, without leaving tell-tale tracks.

The nest is a bulky, untidy cup of dead leaves from sedges, reeds and other waterside species. It is concealed by pulling down reed stems to form a canopy. The 6–12 eggs, laid in April–July, have a creamy-white ground colour, with many small speckles and a few bigger blotches of bluish-grey and rusty-brown. They take about three weeks to hatch into jet-black, downy chicks. Two broods are usual. One parent guards the chicks while the other fetches food, until the chicks are independent at seven to eight weeks.

Location	Behaviour	Sketch
Date		
Time		
Weather	Field marks	
Call		

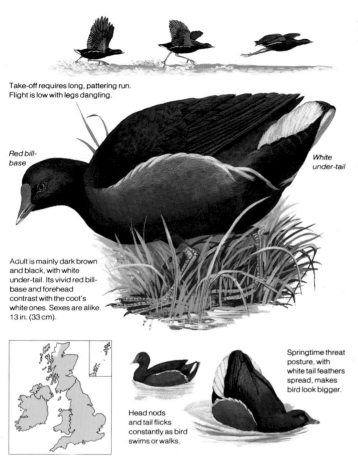

Take-off requires long, pattering run. Flight is low with legs dangling.

Red bill-base

White under-tail

Adult is mainly dark brown and black, with white under-tail. Its vivid red bill-base and forehead contrast with the coot's white ones. Sexes are alike. 13 in. (33 cm).

Present all year; common and widespread.

Head nods and tail flicks constantly as bird swims or walks.

Springtime threat posture, with white tail feathers spread, makes bird look bigger.

Chicks have bare blue crown and black down.

Juvenile is dull brown and pale-faced; tail pattern differs from coot's.

Moorhen *Gallinula chloropus*

In spite of its name, the moorhen is not a moorland bird; 'moor' comes from the Anglo-Saxon word *mor*, meaning mere or bog. The 16th-century naturalist William Turner called the bird 'mot-hen' because the species frequented 'moats which surround the houses of the great'. In fact, moorhens can be found on almost any stretch of fresh water.

The moorhen's food consists of water plants and their fruits and seeds, insects, spiders, worms and other invertebrates. Like the coot, the moorhen is aggressive in defence of its territory, and boundary disputes often lead to exchanges of blows with bill and feet. The moorhen's toes are particularly long, spreading its weight so that it can walk on floating water plants. There is no webbing between the toes, and perhaps because of this, the moorhen's swimming action seems laboured, the head jerking forward with each stroke like a cyclist toiling uphill. The bird swims readily under water, and when very alarmed stays submerged and motionless with only its bill above the surface.

One bird's clutch of eggs is likely to number five to ten, buff in colour with fine reddish-brown speckles. A nest may contain up to 20 eggs, laid by more than one female.

Location	Behaviour	Sketch
Date		
Time		
Weather	Field marks	
Call		

White bill, forehead

Sites Guide

The coot's large nest of reeds is often raised above the level of the water, with a ramp leading from the top to the water.

The species may be seen at sites numbers: 1, 13, 14, 16, 23, 25, 27, 28, 36-40, 42, 44, 46, 48, 51, 60, 62.

Males fight frequently and fiercely when claiming territory.

Juvenile is greyer than young moorhen, with pale throat and breast.

Breeding birds often chase away other species.

Lobed toes

Coot *Fulica atra*

A glimpse of this bird explains the origin of the expression 'as bald as a coot'. In striking contrast to their black plumage, both sexes have an area of bare skin on their foreheads called a frontal shield, matching their glistening white bills.

Males squabble frequently over territory, and the shield plays an important part in their aggressive displays. It is held forward, low on the water, with wings and body feathers fluffed up behind to give as menacing an impression as possible. As the two birds approach one another the coot's harsh, unmusical call – rather like a hammer striking a sheet of metal – rings out.

The coot benefits greatly from booms in the building industry, which demand enormous amounts of sand and gravel for making concrete. The quarrying of these materials usually leaves behind flooded pits which provide excellent homes for many British water birds. In winter, the bigger expanses of water may attract large flocks of coots busily diving for the soft submerged plants that form the bulk of their diet. After a dive, the bird, bobbing up like a cork, brings its food to the surface to eat. The eggs are similar to those of the moorhen, but have more and finer markings. Chicks are independent after eight weeks.

Adult has white bill and frontal shield, contrasting with slate-black plumage. Lobed toes help swimming and diving. Sexes are alike. 15 in. (38 cm).

Long legs trail in flight after pattering take-off.

Present all year; visitors join winter flocks.

Feeding bird jump-dives with a splash, popping up again at same spot.

Chicks have brightly coloured bare heads.

Location	Behaviour	Sketch
Date		
Time		
Weather	Field marks	
Call		

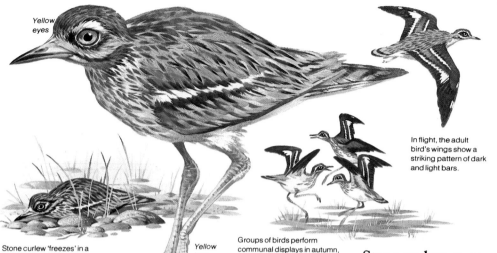

Yellow eyes

In flight, the adult bird's wings show a striking pattern of dark and light bars.

Stone curlew 'freezes' in a flat and concealing posture when taken by surprise, with head and neck stretched out.

Yellow legs

Groups of birds perform communal displays in autumn, leaping wildly and waving their wings frantically.

Adult bird's rounded head, large yellow eyes, yellow legs and white bar on wing are distinctive. Adults and juveniles of both sexes have similar plumage. 16 in. (40 cm).

Mar.–Oct. visitor; rare outside breeding areas.

Courting birds perform a stately ritual, facing in opposite directions, with bills pointed downwards.

Sites Guide

For their breeding grounds, stone curlews favour heaths, downs, stony or sandy areas and open farmland.

The species may be seen at site number: 33.

Stone curlew *Burhinus oedicnemus*

Fluty, wailing and somewhat plaintive, the cry of the stone curlew hangs hauntingly over the chalky downs and sandy heaths of south and east England. The bird owes its name to that call and to its breeding ground; for its 'coooeee' resembles that of the curlew, and it usually nests on stony ground.

Snails, slugs and a variety of insects are the main food of the stone curlew, although it occasionally swallows larger prey such as field-mice and frogs. One reason why the stone curlew favours open country is that it likes to be able to see danger approaching at a distance. Then it usually prefers to run away rather than to fly.

The nest is a shallow scrape on bare ground, at most slightly lined with tiny pebbles, plant oddments or rabbit droppings. The stone curlew arrives on the south coast from March onwards. Breeding begins in April or May, two or rarely three eggs being laid. They are creamy or yellowish-brown, speckled and streaked with brown and grey. Both sexes take turns to incubate the eggs, which hatch after about 26 days. The young are pale buff above and white below, with blackish streaks and speckles on the back, which provide good camouflage.

Location	Behaviour	Sketch
Date		
Time		
Weather	Field marks	
Call		

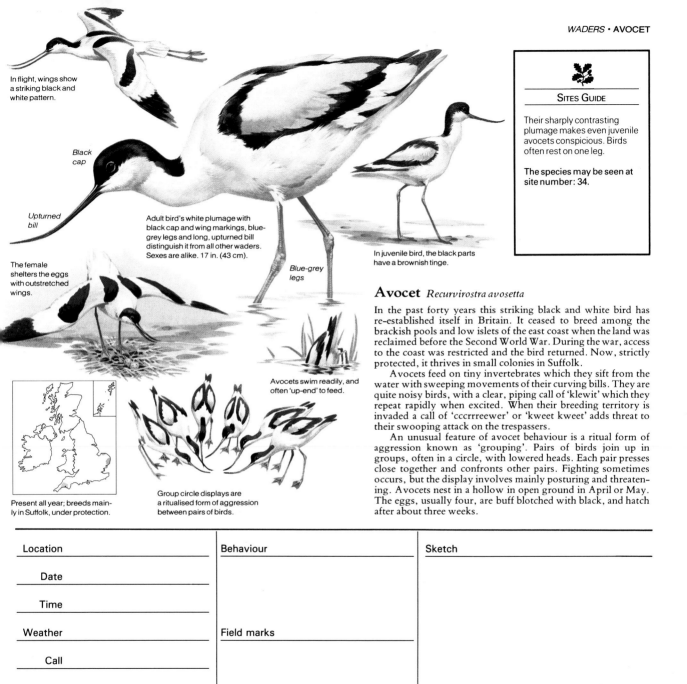

In flight, wings show a striking black and white pattern.

Black cap

Upturned bill

Adult bird's white plumage with black cap and wing markings, blue-grey legs and long, upturned bill distinguish it from all other waders. Sexes are alike. 17 in. (43 cm).

Blue-grey legs

The female shelters the eggs with outstretched wings.

In juvenile bird, the black parts have a brownish tinge.

Avocets swim readily, and often 'up-end' to feed.

Present all year; breeds mainly in Suffolk, under protection.

Group circle displays are a ritualised form of aggression between pairs of birds.

Sites Guide

Their sharply contrasting plumage makes even juvenile avocets conspicuous. Birds often rest on one leg.

The species may be seen at site number: 34.

Avocet *Recurvirostra avosetta*

In the past forty years this striking black and white bird has re-established itself in Britain. It ceased to breed among the brackish pools and low islets of the east coast when the land was reclaimed before the Second World War. During the war, access to the coast was restricted and the bird returned. Now, strictly protected, it thrives in small colonies in Suffolk.

Avocets feed on tiny invertebrates which they sift from the water with sweeping movements of their curving bills. They are quite noisy birds, with a clear, piping call of 'klewit' which they repeat rapidly when excited. When their breeding territory is invaded a call of 'cccrrreewer' or 'kweet kweet' adds threat to their swooping attack on the trespassers.

An unusual feature of avocet behaviour is a ritual form of aggression known as 'grouping'. Pairs of birds join up in groups, often in a circle, with lowered heads. Each pair presses close together and confronts other pairs. Fighting sometimes occurs, but the display involves mainly posturing and threatening. Avocets nest in a hollow in open ground in April or May. The eggs, usually four, are buff blotched with black, and hatch after about three weeks.

Location	Behaviour	Sketch
Date		
Time		
Weather	Field marks	
Call		

Long crest

Adult male

Adult female

In flight, white underparts are conspicuous, and broad rounded wings are unlike those of any other wader.

Chestnut under-tail

Adult male in breeding plumage. Its long crest and striking plumage pattern of black, white and dark, iridescent green are very distinctive. 12 in. (30 cm).

Present all year; in coldest winters most birds migrate.

Sites Guide

The lapwing's nest is a simple scrape in the earth, usually sited on slightly elevated ground and lined with grass. Eggs are well camouflaged against predators.

The species may be seen at sites numbers: 5, 6, 11, 12, 14, 16, 21, 23, 27-29, 32, 36-39, 41, 42, 51, 52.

Lapwing *Vanellus vanellus*

The male lapwing's territorial display flight is one of the most delightful sights of the countryside in spring. Rising from the ground on slowly beating wings it climbs steadily, then goes into a twisting, rolling dive which ends with an upwards twist and a flurry of rapid, buzzing wing-beats. The Anglo-Saxons used the word *hleapewince* – literally 'run' and 'wink' – to describe this twisting flight, and this is the origin of the bird's common name today.

The lapwing is one of the group of waders called plovers, and in some districts is known as the green plover because of its greenish, iridescent back plumage. Countrymen often know it as the 'peewit', after its distinctive 'pee-weet' call. At one time, lapwings were a common sight on ploughed fields and were welcomed by farmers because they devour many pests, especially leatherjackets and wireworms. But the use of insecticides and of farming machinery, which destroys nests, has driven them to meadows and marshes in summer.

In winter, lapwings gather in flocks, often of several hundreds, and move to warmer districts such as south-west England, Ireland or southern Europe.

Location	Behaviour	Sketch
Date		
Time		
Weather	Field marks	
Call		

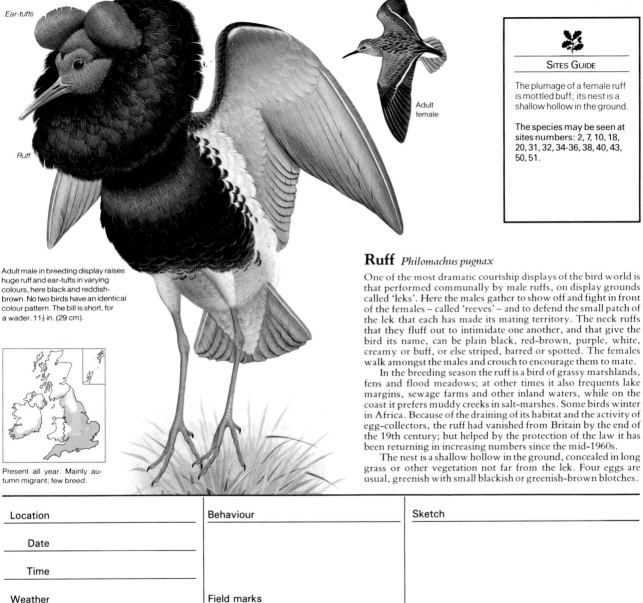

Ear-tufts

Ruff

Adult female

Adult male in breeding display raises huge ruff and ear-tufts in varying colours, here black and reddish-brown. No two birds have an identical colour pattern. The bill is short, for a wader. 11½ in. (29 cm).

Present all year. Mainly autumn migrant; few breed.

Ruff *Philomachus pugnax*

One of the most dramatic courtship displays of the bird world is that performed communally by male ruffs, on display grounds called 'leks'. Here the males gather to show off and fight in front of the females – called 'reeves' – and to defend the small patch of the lek that each has made its mating territory. The neck ruffs that they fluff out to intimidate one another, and that give the bird its name, can be plain black, red-brown, purple, white, creamy or buff, or else striped, barred or spotted. The females walk amongst the males and crouch to encourage them to mate.

In the breeding season the ruff is a bird of grassy marshlands, fens and flood meadows; at other times it also frequents lake margins, sewage farms and other inland waters, while on the coast it prefers muddy creeks in salt-marshes. Some birds winter in Africa. Because of the draining of its habitat and the activity of egg-collectors, the ruff had vanished from Britain by the end of the 19th century; but helped by the protection of the law it has been returning in increasing numbers since the mid-1960s.

The nest is a shallow hollow in the ground, concealed in long grass or other vegetation not far from the lek. Four eggs are usual, greenish with small blackish or greenish-brown blotches.

Location	Behaviour	Sketch
Date		
Time		
Weather	Field marks	
Call		

Long bill

When the bird dives, air rushing over its tail feathers makes a bleating sound.

Adult bird is dark with contrasting light stripes on the crown and back. It has a very long straight bill. Its tail is fringed with reddish-brown and white. Sexes are alike. 10¼ in. (27 cm).

When flushed, the snipe rises and zigzags away with hoarse calls.

Present all year; most numerous in winter.

Snipe nest in tussocks of grass, rushes or other marsh vegetation. The chicks are dark with white speckles.

The bird probes deep in the mud of its marshy habitat for much of its prey. Surface-living insects are also eaten.

Snipe *Gallinago gallinago*

The most remarkable thing about the snipe is the length of its bill, which is about a quarter of the bird's total length. The tip of the bill is flexible and highly sensitive, and this enables the snipe to detect and identify the worms and invertebrates on which it mainly lives. But although it usually 'digs' for its food, it also eats surface-living insects.

The snipe performs a spectacular courtship display. It climbs on rapidly beating wings to heights of from fifty to several hundred feet and then dives with its outer tail feathers spread. The feathers vibrate in the airstream and give out a plaintive, bleating sound. At the end of its shallow dive, the bird climbs again and repeats the performance. When flushed, the snipe's alarm call is a scraping 'scaaap', which it utters as it twists alternately from left to right. The call in the spring is a hollow 'chippa–chippa–chippa'.

The snipe's nest is well hidden on the ground, and the clutch is usually of four pale, greenish-brown eggs with grey and dark brown blotches and speckles. The female incubates the eggs. At first, both parents feed the young. But the chicks soon learn to feed themselves and they can fly when about three weeks old.

Location	Behaviour	Sketch
Date		
Time		
Weather	Field marks	
Call		

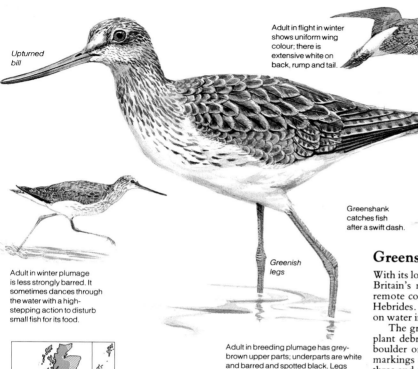

Upturned bill

Adult in flight in winter shows uniform wing colour; there is extensive white on back, rump and tail.

Greenshank catches fish after a swift dash.

Adult in winter plumage is less strongly barred. It sometimes dances through the water with a high-stepping action to disturb small fish for its food.

Greenish legs

Summer migrant in Scotland; elsewhere on passage.

Adult in breeding plumage has grey-brown upper parts; underparts are white and barred and spotted black. Legs and slightly upturned bill are greenish. Sexes are alike. 12 in. (30 cm).

When young or eggs are disturbed, the parent bird fiercely defends them.

Greenshank *Tringa nebularia*

With its long green legs and sleek body, the greenshank is one of Britain's most elegant waders. The species is a bird of wild, remote country, and breeds in the Scottish Highlands and the Hebrides. At dawn and dusk, greenshanks may be seen feeding on water insects on the shores of lochs.

The greenshank's nest is a hollow in the ground lined with plant debris, and is often close to some large object such as a boulder or dead branch. The eggs are creamy-coloured, with markings of dark brown or grey, and they hatch after about three and a half weeks. The chicks are generally brooded by the female for most of the first day; later, they are led to the nearest feeding area. Outside the breeding season the birds may turn up on the banks of rivers, and on marshes, sewage farms and estuaries. In winter they move south to the shores of the Mediterranean and beyond to south of the Sahara desert.

The call of the greenshank is similar to that of its close relative, the redshank, but it is a shorter call, more staccato and less musical – a ringing 'tew-tew-tew'. Apart from the colour of its legs, the greenshank differs from the redshank in being larger and greyer, and in lacking white wing-patches.

Location	Behaviour	Sketch
Date		
Time		
Weather	Field marks	
Call		

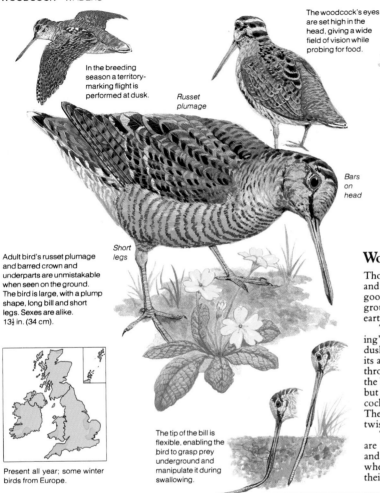

In the breeding season a territory-marking flight is performed at dusk.

Russet plumage

The woodcock's eyes are set high in the head, giving a wide field of vision while probing for food.

Bars on head

When flushed from cover, the woodcock takes to the air and swerves adroitly among the trees to evade enemies.

Adult bird's russet plumage and barred crown and underparts are unmistakable when seen on the ground. The bird is large, with a plump shape, long bill and short legs. Sexes are alike. 13½ in. (34 cm).

Short legs

Present all year; some winter birds from Europe.

The tip of the bill is flexible, enabling the bird to grasp prey underground and manipulate it during swallowing.

SITES GUIDE

Blending with its surroundings, a parent woodcock may be almost invisible as it tends its nest among the undergrowth.

The species may be seen at sites numbers: 3, 12-14, 19, 21, 23, 24, 27-30, 37, 38, 43, 44, 47, 49, 51, 54.

Woodcock *Scolopax rusticola*

Though it is a wader, the woodcock has deserted open marshes and taken to damp woodland with open clearings and rides and a good growth of bracken and bramble. Woodcocks need soft ground in which to feed, probing with their long bills for earthworms, insects and their larvae, centipedes and spiders.

The territorial display flight of the woodcock, called 'roding', is very distinctive. The male bird flies over its territory at dusk, covering a wide area on slow-beating wings which belie its actual speed of flight. From time to time it utters two calls, a throaty 'og-og-og' with the bill closed and a 'chee-wick' with the bill open. The first call is barely audible except at close range, but the second carries for a considerable distance. The woodcock's escape flight, when flushed from cover, is very different. Then it moves rapidly among the trees with deftly executed twists and turns.

The nest is a leaf-lined scrape in the ground. The eggs, which are pale fawn speckled with brown and grey, take between 20 and 23 days to hatch. The chicks are tended by both parents, and when danger threatens the parent birds usually squat and rely on their natural camouflage to prevent discovery.

Location	Behaviour	Sketch
Date		
Time		
Weather	Field marks	
Call		

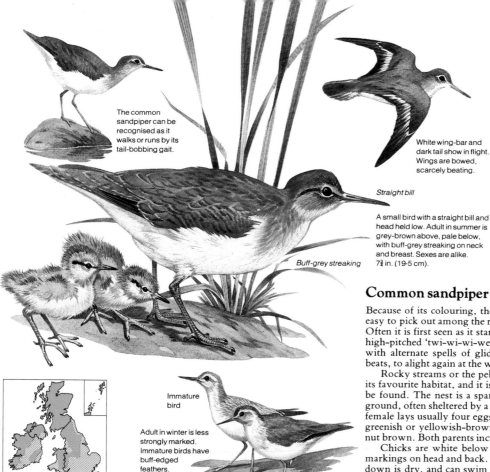

The common sandpiper can be recognised as it walks or runs by its tail-bobbing gait.

White wing-bar and dark tail show in flight. Wings are bowed, scarcely beating.

Straight bill

A small bird with a straight bill and head held low. Adult in summer is grey-brown above, pale below, with buff-grey streaking on neck and breast. Sexes are alike. 7¾ in. (19·5 cm).

Buff-grey streaking

Immature bird

Adult in winter is less strongly marked. Immature birds have buff-edged feathers.

Adult, winter

Apr.–Oct. visitor; a few remain in winter.

The long beak of the common sandpiper is used for probing in the mud beside water for small shellfish, frogs and worms.

The species may be seen at sites numbers: 7, 10, 16, 21, 25, 26, 28, 36-39, 41, 42, 44, 47, 51, 52.

Common sandpiper *Actitis hypoleucos*

Because of its colouring, the common sandpiper is not always easy to pick out among the rocks and stones of a lake shoreline. Often it is first seen as it starts into flight with a loud, musical, high-pitched 'twi-wi-wi-wee', flying low just above the water with alternate spells of gliding and flickering shallow wing-beats, to alight again at the water's edge some distance away.

Rocky streams or the pebbly shore of a lake or reservoir are its favourite habitat, and it is often common where these are to be found. The nest is a sparsely lined hollow or scrape in the ground, often sheltered by a plant or bush. About mid-May the female lays usually four eggs, which vary from creamy-buff to greenish or yellowish-brown, stippled or speckled with chest-nut brown. Both parents incubate them for 20–23 days.

Chicks are white below and buff above, with a few dark markings on head and back. They leave the nest as soon as their down is dry, and can swim and feed almost at once, including diving and swimming under water to escape enemies. When about two weeks old they begin flying, and are fully airborne at three weeks old. At four weeks they are completely independent. In winter most birds migrate south to Africa.

Location	Behaviour	Sketch
Date		
Time		
Weather	Field marks	
Call		

Adult in winter.

Adult in summer.

Straight bill

In flight, black and white tail and broad white wing-bar identify the bird in summer and winter.

Black tail

Adult in summer plumage. White under-tail coverts and black tail distinguish this bird from bar-tailed godwit in breeding season. Bill is straight; bird often wades deeply. Sexes are alike. 16 in. (40 cm).

Present all year. Some breed; most migrants or visitors.

Display postures of male during courtship include wing and tail spreading.

Adult bird in winter plumage. Upper parts are more uniform than in bar-tailed godwit, and legs are longer.

Black-tailed godwit prefers swampy inland grasslands as its breeding ground.

Sites Guide

Flocks of black-tailed godwits are often seen in winter in estuaries on the south coast of England and Ireland.

The species may be seen at sites numbers: 5, 10, 32, 34-36, 47, 59, 64.

Black-tailed godwit *Limosa limosa*

Along with the avocet and the ruff, the black-tailed godwit is one of the few species recently re-established in Britain as breeding birds. In 1953 only four breeding pairs were recorded on the Ouse Washes. Thanks to the efforts of conservationists, the population had increased in the early 1970s to more than 60 pairs. At the same time, the winter migrant population has risen to more than 4,000 birds.

Until the beginning of the 19th century, the black-tailed godwit was widespread in East Anglia and parts of Yorkshire. By 1830 it had almost disappeared because of extensive drainage, and probably also organised shoots and egg-collecting.

Breeding males fly with rapid wing-beats to a height of about 200 ft (60 m), uttering a loud 'tur-ee-tur' that changes at the peak of the ascent to 'crrweetew . . . crrweetew'. At this point the wing-beats slow down and the bird twists from side to side before silently gliding downwards. It completes the display with a final steep dive, with wings almost closed, to the ground. The nest is in a hollow among thick grass; usually four light green eggs are laid, and both parents incubate them for about three weeks. The young fly at about one month old.

Location	Behaviour	Sketch
Date		
Time		
Weather	Field marks	
Call		

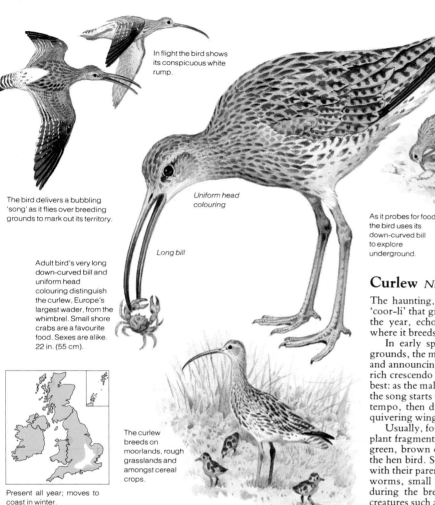

In flight the bird shows its conspicuous white rump.

The bird delivers a bubbling 'song' as it flies over breeding grounds to mark out its territory.

Uniform head colouring

Long bill

Adult bird's very long down-curved bill and uniform head colouring distinguish the curlew, Europe's largest wader, from the whimbrel. Small shore crabs are a favourite food. Sexes are alike. 22 in. (55 cm).

Present all year; moves to coast in winter.

The curlew breeds on moorlands, rough grasslands and amongst cereal crops.

As it probes for food, the bird uses its down-curved bill to explore underground.

SITES GUIDE

Curlews gather at regular roosts on the shore, often in the company of other waders such as oystercatchers.

The species may be seen at sites numbers: 5, 8, 10, 12, 20, 28, 35, 38, 42, 44, 49, 51, 52.

Curlew *Numenius arquata*

The haunting, melancholy call of the curlew – the plaintive 'coor-li' that gives the bird its name – can be heard for most of the year, echoing across windswept moors and marshlands where it breeds, or above the coastal mud-flats in winter.

In early spring, when the birds arrive at their breeding grounds, the males establish their territories, circling a wide area and announcing their presence loud and clear. This is when the rich crescendo of notes which is the curlew's song is heard at its best: as the male rises steeply into the air with rapid wing-beats, the song starts with low-pitched notes and rises both in tone and tempo, then dies away as the bird glides gracefully down on quivering wings.

Usually, four eggs are laid in a shallow depression lined with plant fragments. The eggs are pale green in colour, with darker green, brown or purple blotches, and are incubated mainly by the hen bird. Soon after hatching the young birds leave the nest with their parents. They fly when five or six weeks old. Insects, worms, small frogs and snails form most of the curlew's diet during the breeding season, but in winter it feeds on shore creatures such as crabs, shrimps and cockles.

Location	Behaviour	Sketch
Date		
Time		
Weather	Field marks	
Call		

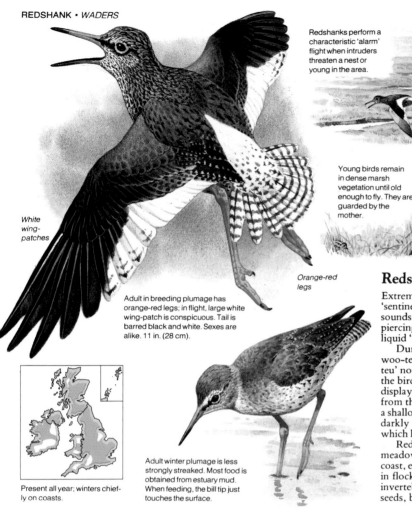

White wing-patches

Redshanks perform a characteristic 'alarm' flight when intruders threaten a nest or young in the area.

Young birds remain in dense marsh vegetation until old enough to fly. They are guarded by the mother.

Orange-red legs

Adult in breeding plumage has orange-red legs; in flight, large white wing-patch is conspicuous. Tail is barred black and white. Sexes are alike. 11 in. (28 cm).

Present all year; winters chiefly on coasts.

Adult winter plumage is less strongly streaked. Most food is obtained from estuary mud. When feeding, the bill tip just touches the surface.

Sites Guide

Redshanks and dunlins may be seen gathered together on the tideline in winter as they feed on marine life such as shellfish.

The species may be seen at sites numbers: 5, 7, 8, 12, 25, 32, 36, 38, 41, 44, 51.

Redshank *Tringa totanus*

Extreme alertness has earned the redshank the description of 'sentinel of the marsh'. A hysterical volley of harsh, piping notes sounds the alarm as soon as any intruder approaches. This piercing warning contrasts sharply with the bird's musical and liquid 'tew-ew-ew' call at other times.

During its display flight the redshank utters a fluting 'tee-woo-tee-woo-tee-woo' song or a long succession of 'teu, teu, teu' notes as it rises and falls on quivering wings. On alighting, the bird often leaves its wings stretched vertically over its back, displaying the white undersides. The redshank begins to breed from the middle of April onwards, nesting amongst the grass in a shallow, lined hollow in the ground. There it lays three or four darkly speckled, creamy eggs. Both adults incubate the eggs, which hatch after about three and a half weeks.

Redshanks inhabit a variety of grassy meadows, river meadows and marshes. When winter comes many move to the coast, especially to the salt-marshes where they often congregate in flocks many hundreds strong. The birds live off all sorts of invertebrates, some small fish and frogs, and a certain amount of seeds, buds and berries.

Location	Behaviour	Sketch
Date		
Time		
Weather	Field marks	
Call		

Brown head

Immature bird

Adult, winter

Dark red bill

Wings have white fore-edge, black tips, all year. Immature birds have darkish band across wing.

Adult in breeding plumage. The 'black' head (in fact chocolate brown) is distinctive, as are the dark red bill and legs. Sexes are alike. 14–15 in. (36–38 cm).

Adult in winter: all that remains of the dark hood of its breeding plumage is a dark spot behind the eye.

Young birds have more grey in plumage than larger gull species at the same age.

Flocks of birds follow ploughs and harrows to capture insects exposed in the turned-up soil.

Present all year; many birds from Europe winter here.

SITES GUIDE

In southern Britain, inland sites such as reservoirs are the most popular homes for colonies of black-headed gulls.

The species may be seen at sites numbers: 12-14, 21, 29, 41, 43, 44, 46, 49, 51, 52, 55, 63.

Black-headed gull *Larus ridibundus*

Of all the British gulls, the black-headed gull least deserves the description of 'sea-gull'. A recent survey showed that out of a total British population of some 300,000 pairs, only about a quarter nested on the coast. Meanwhile numerous colonies, some numbering many thousands of birds, were found inland, particularly in the north, usually in boggy areas around lakes.

In the south a higher proportion of colonies are on the coast, especially on salt marshes or among sand dunes. But even in the south the black-headed gull sometimes nests inland, on gravel or clay pits or on sewage farms.

The voice of the black-headed gull consists of a series of extremely harsh and rasping notes, and the sound of a colony in full cry is overpowering. The nest is a slight platform of vegetation or a sparsely lined scrape in the ground. There are normally three eggs, laid daily from mid-April onwards. Both parents incubate the eggs, for a total period of slightly more than three weeks. If danger threatens, the adults give the alarm and the young hide in the nearest cover or flatten motionless on the ground. The black-headed gull will eat almost anything, from fish and worms to grass, seaweed and refuse.

Location	Behaviour	Sketch
Date		
Time		
Weather	Field marks	
Call		

Thin bill

Barred below

Adult bird in normal grey plumage. Underparts are lighter in colour than upper parts, and heavily barred. Tail is long and rounded, with white patches. Head is small and bill thin. Legs are yellow. Sexes are usually alike, but a few females are brown. 13 in. (33 cm).

Apr.–Aug. visitor; widespread throughout Britain.

Rounded tail

SITES GUIDE

The cuckoo's song inspired the 16th-century poet Edmund Spenser to write of 'The merry cuckoo, messenger of Spring'. It favours wooded areas.

The species may be seen at sites numbers: 6, 8, 12, 17, 19, 22-25, 27, 28, 33, 37, 38, 42.

Cuckoo *Cuculus canorus*

Each April the most eagerly awaited bird-call is that of the cuckoo, a sure sign that summer is on its way. The male bird announces his presence from a high perch and at great length, using the same monotonous but musical notes – 'coo-coo'. The female's call consists of an explosive, bubbling chuckle. Although mid-April is the likeliest time to hear the first cuckoo, some birds arrive from Africa towards the end of March.

The parasitic breeding habits of the cuckoo are notorious. From late May onwards the female flies over her chosen territory in search of foster-homes for her young. She selects a nest belonging to a pair of small birds – such as reed warblers – and deposits a single egg in it. Altogether, she may lay as many as 12 eggs in 12 different nests. Sometimes the eggs closely resemble those of the host bird: this is a natural adaptation and the female is not able to alter the colour and markings at will.

Since the mid-1940s there has been a widespread decrease in the cuckoo population. Reasons for this probably include the destruction of much of its habitat, including hedgerows; the increasing use of insecticides, which kill off its food; and the tendency towards colder, wetter, springs and summers.

Location	Behaviour	Sketch
Date		
Time		
Weather	Field marks	
Call		

When threatened, the adult bird flattens itself defensively on a barn floor, its wings spread horizontally. Its long-necked nestlings shelter behind it.

White face

Hollow elms are a favourite nest site with the barn owl, but they are fast disappearing from the countryside.

White underparts

Present all year; scarce in parts of eastern Britain.

Adult has white underparts, and golden-buff upper parts mottled with grey. It has a white heart-shaped face and long legs. Sexes are alike. 13½ in. (34 cm).

Seen from above, the barn owl looks pure white. It systematically patrols fields at night in search of prey upon which to pounce.

SITES GUIDE

The barn owl preys mainly on rats, mice and voles, which it usually hunts at night and carries off to its nest.

The species may be seen at sites numbers: 19, 24, 25, 43, 44, 54.

Barn owl *Tyto alba*

A barn owl's hoarse, eerie, prolonged shriek, often uttered in flight, still has the power to strike a chill into the hearts of those who recall the owl's reputation over the centuries as a bird of ill omen. Geoffrey Chaucer, in the 14th century, referred to the bird as a 'prophet of woe and mischance'.

Year after year many barn owls return to established roosts and breeding sites in old barns, ruins and exposed buildings such as church towers. The birds also inhabit natural holes in trees and cliffs. Often the location of these sites is revealed by large accumulations of castings or pellets, the indigestible remains of the birds' prey.

The breeding season is a long one, starting in February or March. Sometimes there are two broods. The size of each clutch of white eggs varies from three to 11, depending on the food available, but four to seven is the average. The male feeds the female during the 32–34 days of incubation. Young birds have two coats of down, the first white, the second, after 12 days, creamy. Like adult birds, the young make various hissing and snoring noises, but if disturbed in the nest they snap their bills together loudly. They fly at eight to ten weeks old.

Location	Behaviour	Sketch
Date		
Time		
Weather	Field marks	
Call		

The little owl's flight is low, swift and strongly undulating.

Yellow eyes

Fence posts and tree stumps are favourite day-time perches.

Fledgelings, when anxious, bob their heads in a comical manner.

Present all year; derived from 19th-century introductions.

Holes and crevices in old buildings are sometimes used as nesting sites. The eggs are incubated by the female.

Its small size, yellow eyes and 'frowning' expression identify the little owl. Insects such as dor-beetles are its main prey. Sexes are alike. 8½ in. (22 cm).

Little owl *Athene noctua*

Warm spring evenings are the best time to listen for the call of the little owl: a long, musical but plaintive mewing 'kiew', repeated at widely spaced intervals. Occasionally the call is interspersed with a more excited, yelping 'werrrow'. The place to listen is on agricultural land where there are plenty of hollow trees and farm buildings, which provide nesting sites. Little owls can also be found in parkland, old orchards and quarries, and on sea cliffs.

The little owl was introduced to Britain from the Continent during the last century. By the early part of the 20th century it was widespread, breeding throughout most of England south of Yorkshire, except for the West Country. Wales was also partly colonised.

From mid-April onwards the single clutch of three to five eggs is laid on the bare floor of the nest cavity. The chicks hatch after about a month, and are at first clothed in thick, short, white down. Both adults feed them. They leave the nest often up to a week before they can fly well at five weeks old. The bird's diet consists largely of earthworms, molluscs and insects – particularly beetles – and some small mammals.

Location		Behaviour	Sketch
Date			
Time			
Weather		Field marks	
Call			

Long, barred wings have dark patches at 'wrists' on both upper and lower surfaces, contrasting with the pale primary feathers.

Underparts, seen in flight, are dark at the front and pale at the rear. Tail bars are fewer but bolder than those of the long-eared owl. Sexes are alike. 15 in. (38 cm).

Pale rear

A semi-horizontal stance is often adopted when perching.

Present all year; more widespread in winter.

Dark front

Display flight includes a loud clapping made as the wingtips meet below the body.

The short-eared owl nests on the ground; the young move away before they can fly.

Short-eared owl *Asio flammeus*

The short-eared owl hunts by low-level searching, its sensitive ears enabling it to pinpoint the faintest rustle in the grass as it covers rough grasslands and other open country in search of prey. The bird is immediately identified by its wing-beats which are like those of an enormous moth, the wings passing through a large arc.

The bird hunts in daylight or at dusk in treeless country, chiefly in upland Wales, the Pennines and Scotland. Some breeding pairs occur in suitable country in Kent and East Anglia.

Breeding begins from April onwards. Three to eight white eggs are laid in a shallow, unlined hollow on the ground among long grass or heather. The eggs are laid at intervals of two days or more; incubation starts with the first egg laid and lasts for 24–28 days. The chicks, clad all over in thick creamy-buff down, are fed by the female with small rodents such as short-tailed voles, and also with shrews, small birds and insects brought by the male. The short-eared owl is usually silent except when the nest is approached too closely, when a shrill 'keeorr' may be heard. The British population is joined by migrant birds from the Continent.

Location	Behaviour	Sketch
Date		
Time		
Weather	Field marks	
Call		

In flight, the black patches on the wing 'wrists' are less strongly marked than those of the short-eared owl. The tail has tiny bars, and the underparts are darkish.

Ear-opening on left is slightly behind that on right. Sounds reach one ear before the other; time-lag enables owl to pin-point the source.

Present all year; local, and no-where common.

Ear-tufts

The long-eared owl's ear-tufts and distinctive face pattern identify it when seen roosting by day. Sexes are alike. 13½ in. (34 cm.)

When anxious, the bird draws its body up into a stiff, slender posture.

SITES GUIDE

To frighten off intruders at the nest, an adult long-eared owl droops its wings and raises its back feathers to frame its head.

The species may be seen at sites numbers: 24, 28, 47, 48, 51, 54.

Long-eared owl *Asio otus*

Although the most conspicuous features of the long-eared owl are its 'ears', they are in fact no more than tufts of feathers; the actual ear openings are situated at the sides of the head. Active only at night, this owl spends the day roosting in dense tree cover, when it is easily overlooked by the casual observer. It lives in coniferous woodland, plantations, small copses and clumps of trees in farmland and moorland.

The bird's main call is a low, drawn-out 'oooo' repeated three times every few seconds. It has considerable carrying power, and can be heard up to half a mile away. The chicks have a curious call, like a creaking gate hinge.

Breeding begins at any time from late February onwards, and the courtship display involves wing clapping and flying with slow, exaggerated wing-beats. The pure white eggs – three to eight in number, but usually four or five – are laid on alternate days in an old nest of some other large bird, or in a squirrel's drey, or very occasionally on the ground at the foot of a tree or amongst heather. The female normally incubates the eggs for 25–30 days, and feeds the hatched young with food brought by the male. The chicks fledge at 23 or 24 days old.

Location	Behaviour	Sketch
Date		
Time		
Weather	Field marks	
Call		

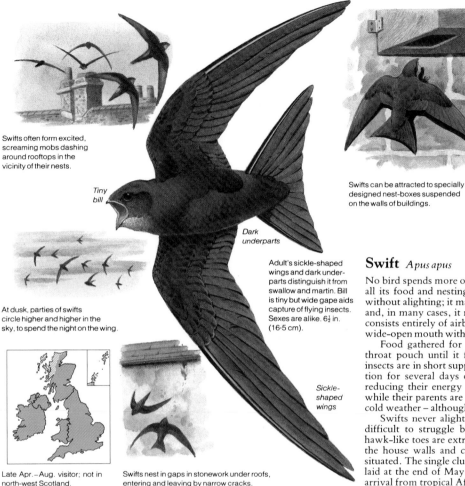

Swifts often form excited, screaming mobs dashing around rooftops in the vicinity of their nests.

Tiny bill

Dark underparts

At dusk, parties of swifts circle higher and higher in the sky, to spend the night on the wing.

Late Apr.–Aug. visitor; not in north-west Scotland.

Adult's sickle-shaped wings and dark underparts distinguish it from swallow and martin. Bill is tiny but wide gape aids capture of flying insects. Sexes are alike. 6½ in. (16·5 cm).

Sickle-shaped wings

Swifts nest in gaps in stonework under roofs, entering and leaving by narrow cracks.

Swifts can be attracted to specially designed nest-boxes suspended on the walls of buildings.

SITES GUIDE

Young swifts have pale feather edges. Their shallow nest is of fine plant material stuck together with their parents' saliva.

This bird is widespread, and may be seen at the majority of sites within the range indicated by the map on this page.

Swift *Apus apus*

No bird spends more of its life in the air than the swift. It collects all its food and nesting material in flight; it drinks and bathes without alighting; it mates and can spend the night on the wing; and, in many cases, it manages to outfly birds of prey. Its food consists entirely of airborne insects which are funnelled into its wide-open mouth with the help of the surrounding stiff bristles.

Food gathered for the young is accumulated in the bird's throat pouch until it forms a large, compacted bulge. When insects are in short supply, the chicks can survive partial starvation for several days or even weeks by becoming torpid, so reducing their energy loss. Before their feathers develop, and while their parents are out hunting, they can even survive quite cold weather – although they become sluggish at such times.

Swifts never alight on the ground voluntarily, and find it difficult to struggle back into the air if they do. But their hawk-like toes are extremely strong, enabling them to cling to the house walls and cliff faces on which their nest holes are situated. The single clutch of two or three smooth, white eggs is laid at the end of May or the beginning of June, on the adults' arrival from tropical Africa.

Location	Behaviour	Sketch
Date		
Time		
Weather	Field marks	
Call		

Grey-brown plumage

Adult male has soft, grey-brown plumage. Slow beating of long wings is characteristic. Bill is small, but as it is opened, lower jaw becomes wider, giving wide gape for catching insects. 10½ in. (27 cm).

Wide gape

When perching, bird is usually aligned along the branch rather than across it.

Nightjars are usually seen in flight at dusk, gliding and banking erratically but buoyantly.

May – Oct. visitor; commonest East Anglia and the south.

Female lacks white wing-spots and tail-spots of male. The nest is no more than a scrape in the ground.

Nightjar *Caprimulgus europaeus*

Its extraordinary churring-jarring song, heard mostly at night, gives the nightjar its name. The sound is rather like that of a small engine revving rapidly for stretches of up to five minutes, with an alternating rise and fall in pitch. During this performance, the bird is usually perched lengthwise along a dead branch – though it sometimes delivers its song from a leafy branch, or even from the ground or in flight. By contrast, the call note is a simple 'cooic'.

On arriving from the southern half of Africa in the spring, the nightjar takes up territory in open woodland, heathland, moorland or coastal sand-dunes. During the day, the birds are almost invisible as they lie motionless on the ground and, from a distance, they are often mistaken for bunches of dead leaves. They lay their eggs on bare ground, often near dead wood, and this makes a sitting bird even harder to see.

The clutch of two eggs is laid from about mid-May onwards. Both parents take part in incubation, but the hen only does so during the day. Both birds feed the chicks until the female starts to incubate her second clutch, when the male manages alone. After dusk, the nightjar feeds on flying insects.

Location	Behaviour	Sketch
Date		
Time		
Weather	Field marks	
Call		

In flight, short wings and tail and brilliant blue-green back are clearly visible. Flight is low, straight and swift, with rapid wing-beats.

Iridescent blue-green above

Adult male is a distinctive, stockily built bird with a large head, iridescent blue-green upper parts and orange-chestnut cheeks and underparts. It has a white throat and neck-patch, red feet and a long, dagger-like bill. Sexes are alike. 6½ in. (16·5 cm).

Orange-chestnut below

Red feet

Present all year; some move to coast in winter.

Sites Guide

The kingfisher often chooses a branch above the water for a perch from which to dive after its prey, and a post against which to kill the fish before eating it.

The species may be seen at sites numbers: 3, 7, 13, 14, 16, 19, 21, 25-28, 32, 34, 36, 37, 42, 44, 54.

Kingfisher *Alcedo atthis*

Few birds are shyer than the kingfisher, so that birdwatchers rarely have a close view of it. The most that many people see of this beautifully coloured bird is a brief glimpse as it flashes past them – a swift arrow of colour speeding along the river bank. Frequently, the first indication of the bird's presence is its call: a loud, shrill, piping 'cheeeee' or 'chikeeee'.

The kingfisher spends all year in Britain, and suffers severely in cold winters when its food supply is literally cut off from it. Rivers and lakes ice over, and the bird cannot get at its usual diet of small fish and aquatic insects. At such times the kingfisher may move to coastal rock pools and creeks, where it has a better chance of survival.

Both male and female dig the burrow in which the nest is placed. The nest is gradually littered with an accumulation of regurgitated fish bones. Both birds incubate the eggs. The young are hatched after about three weeks and spend nearly four weeks in the nest. The adults get very dirty while moving in and out of the tunnel and frequently clean themselves by plunging into the adjacent stream. The kingfisher is seldom preyed upon by other birds, as its flesh has an unpleasant taste.

Location	Behaviour	Sketch
Date		
Time		
Weather	Field marks	
Call		

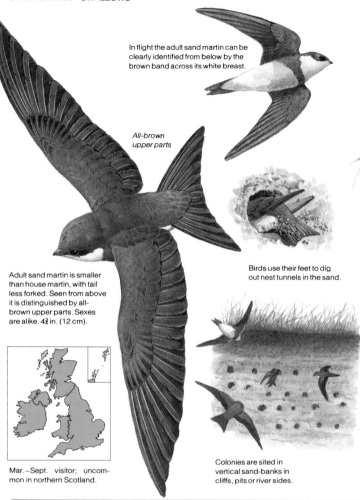

In flight the adult sand martin can be clearly identified from below by the brown band across its white breast.

All-brown upper parts

Adult sand martin is smaller than house martin, with tail less forked. Seen from above it is distinguished by all-brown upper parts. Sexes are alike. 4¾ in. (12 cm).

Mar.–Sept. visitor; uncommon in northern Scotland.

Birds use their feet to dig out nest tunnels in the sand.

Colonies are sited in vertical sand-banks in cliffs, pits or river sides.

Sand martins roost in reed beds, often congregating in large numbers at dusk.

Sand martin *Riparia riparia*

Sand martins take their name from their nesting habits, for they scrape out horizontal tunnels 24–36 in. (60–90 cm) long in sand-banks and enlarge them at the end to form a nesting chamber. Industrial man has provided them with plenty of nesting sites such as railway cuttings or sand and gravel quarries; but lacking these they use river banks, soft sea-cliffs or ready-made holes.

The nesting chamber is lined with plant material and feathers picked up in flight. Breeding starts in mid-May in the south, and there are usually four or five eggs in a clutch; as with many hole-nesting birds the eggs are pure white, probably so that they can be located in the dark. Both parents share incubation, which takes 12–16 days. At first the chicks are fed by both adults in the nest itself, but later they come to the burrow entrance. After about 19 days they take to the air. Sand martins fly south to equatorial West Africa in August or September. They gather in thousands in communal roosts before migrating.

Like swallows, sand martins feed on insects on the wing, often over water, but their flight lacks the swallow's easy grace. They have a hard, twittering call.

Location	Behaviour	Sketch
Date		
Time		
Weather	Field marks	
Call		

Russet throat

Female

Male

Adult male's russet throat and long tail streamers are unmistakable. Upper parts are bluish-black, and there are white spots on the tail. Adult female has shorter tail streamers and is generally duller. 7½ in. (19 cm).

Long tail streamers

Mar.–Oct. visitor; widespread; none in cities.

Swallow *Hirundo rustica*

The old country saying that 'one swallow doesn't make a summer' is more justified than many of its kind. For although the swallow is popularly regarded as a harbinger of summer, the first birds may appear from their South African wintering grounds as early as the beginning of March. Adult birds usually return to the same locality where they bred the previous year – often to exactly the same site. Throughout the summer breeding season the swallow's pleasant twittering warble may be heard well before sunrise, from a bird in flight or from a perch.

When men lived in caves swallows probably did the same; nowadays they have adapted to nesting in buildings and under bridges. Usually, each of the two or three clutches produced in a year consists of three to six eggs, glossy white with a speckling of pinkish-brown or pale grey.

In autumn, adults and young birds head for the South African sun, feeding off insects caught on the wing. It was once thought that when swallows disappeared in autumn they had buried themselves in the mud of rivers and ponds: an idea doubtless fostered by the fact that the birds often congregate in such places just before they migrate.

Location	Behaviour	Sketch
Date		
Time		
Weather	Field marks	
Call		

Crest

Buff eye-stripes

In flight, white wing marks, dark outer tail feathers and white nape band distinguish the woodlark from the skylark.

The bird usually delivers its mellow song in a circular song flight.

Short tail

Woodlark has shorter tail and more richly patterned plumage than skylark, and has buffish eye-stripes meeting across the nape. There is a small crest. Sexes are alike. 6 in. (15 cm).

Partial migrant; scarce, decreased in recent years.

Normally the woodlark feeds on insects, but in autumn it eats seeds.

SITES GUIDE

The woodlark's nest is a neat cup of grass, moss and roots built on the ground and lined with horsehair and other fine material.

This bird is vulnerable to public pressure at its breeding sites, and for this reason no specific geographical references are given.

Woodlark *Lullula arborea*

The song of the woodlark is highly distinctive – a rich, sweet, mellow medley, consisting of varied phrases of one or more notes repeated several times, and interspersed with an occasional 'loo-loo-loo', from which the bird's generic name is derived. The song is delivered from a tree or bush, or during the song flight. In this, the male spirals higher and higher in wide circles, then gradually drops back. Occasionally the bird falls silent at about 100 ft, then plummets with closed wings almost to the ground, opening its wings as brakes just before it alights. Although a bird of open terrain, like the skylark, the woodlark favours land with scattered trees.

Three or four eggs are laid, usually in early April. They are similar in colour to those of the skylark. Incubation takes 12–16 days. Both parents feed the chicks, which leave the nest after 11–12 days, a few days before they can fly properly.

At the beginning of the 19th century, woodlarks were said to breed in virtually every county in England and Wales, but now they are scarce. The cold winters of 1961–2 and 1962–3 decimated them. More recent declines may be due to loss of habitat through afforestation and more intensive agriculture.

Location	Behaviour	Sketch
Date		
Time		
Weather	Field marks	
Call		

Parties of migrating birds are seen on open ground such as sand-dunes.

The skylark has a sustained song flight. The bird often delivers its song while hovering; but it may also sing as it rises, descends or perches.

Crest

Shore lark
Eremophila alpestris

Yellow and black face pattern, black collar and black 'horns' of male distinguish the shore lark from other larks. It has a characteristic 'tseep' call.

Long tail

Present all year; winter migrants from northern Europe.

Skylark is larger and browner than woodlark, with white outer tail feathers. It has a slight crest. Sexes are alike. 7 in. (18 cm).

Skylark *Alauda arvensis*

Though the skylark's plumage is sombre and its song not particularly fine, it is not hard to see why this bird became a favourite of poets and composers. As it performs its conspicuous flight above the open fields and downs, giving voice loudly and constantly, it is a difficult bird to ignore. It is very much identified with the countryside rather than with towns; moreover, it breeds more widely than any other bird in Britain, so is seen in all parts of the country that suit it – farmland, grassland, meadows, sand-dunes and commons.

The skylark rises several hundred feet vertically in hovering flight, sustaining its clear warbling song for several minutes at a time. Then the bird sinks down, singing until it is near the ground. Between three and five eggs are generally laid, in colour off-white or very pale green, heavily speckled with brown or olive. The chicks depend on camouflage and thick ground cover for protection, for they do not fly well until they are about three weeks old. Food is mainly seeds, insects and their larvae.

The shore lark, a visitor from Scandinavia, is a bird of dry, stony and sandy tracts in the Arctic and above the tree line in northern mountains.

Location	Behaviour	Sketch
Date		
Time		
Weather	Field marks	
Call		

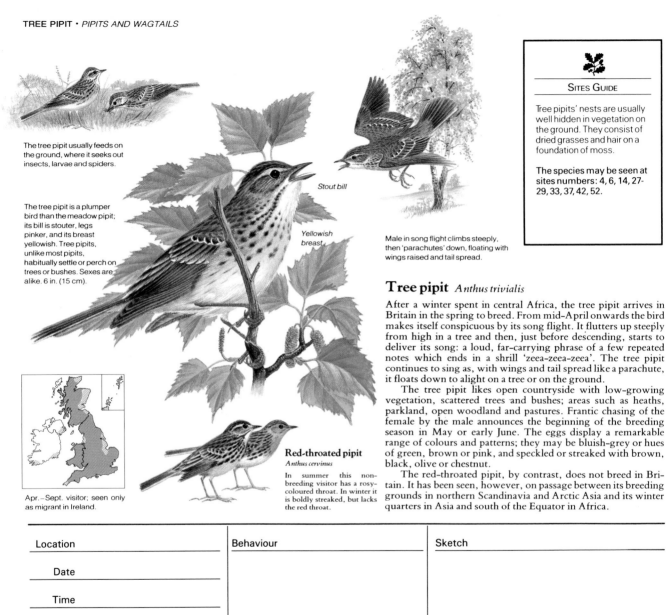

The tree pipit usually feeds on the ground, where it seeks out insects, larvae and spiders.

The tree pipit is a plumper bird than the meadow pipit; its bill is stouter, legs pinker, and its breast yellowish. Tree pipits, unlike most pipits, habitually settle or perch on trees or bushes. Sexes are alike. 6 in. (15 cm).

Stout bill

Yellowish breast

Male in song flight climbs steeply, then 'parachutes' down, floating with wings raised and tail spread.

Apr.–Sept. visitor; seen only as migrant in Ireland.

Red-throated pipit
Anthus cervinus
In summer this non-breeding visitor has a rosy-coloured throat. In winter it is boldly streaked, but lacks the red throat.

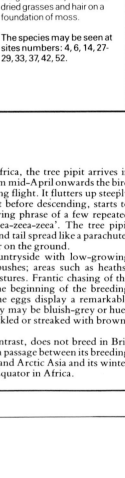

SITES GUIDE

Tree pipits' nests are usually well hidden in vegetation on the ground. They consist of dried grasses and hair on a foundation of moss.

The species may be seen at sites numbers: 4, 6, 14, 27-29, 33, 37, 42, 52.

Tree pipit *Anthus trivialis*

After a winter spent in central Africa, the tree pipit arrives in Britain in the spring to breed. From mid-April onwards the bird makes itself conspicuous by its song flight. It flutters up steeply from high in a tree and then, just before descending, starts to deliver its song: a loud, far-carrying phrase of a few repeated notes which ends in a shrill 'zeea-zeea-zeea'. The tree pipit continues to sing as, with wings and tail spread like a parachute, it floats down to alight on a tree or on the ground.

The tree pipit likes open countryside with low-growing vegetation, scattered trees and bushes; areas such as heaths, parkland, open woodland and pastures. Frantic chasing of the female by the male announces the beginning of the breeding season in May or early June. The eggs display a remarkable range of colours and patterns; they may be bluish-grey or hues of green, brown or pink, and speckled or streaked with brown, black, olive or chestnut.

The red-throated pipit, by contrast, does not breed in Britain. It has been seen, however, on passage between its breeding grounds in northern Scandinavia and Arctic Asia and its winter quarters in Asia and south of the Equator in Africa.

Location	Behaviour	Sketch
Date		
Time		
Weather	Field marks	
Call		

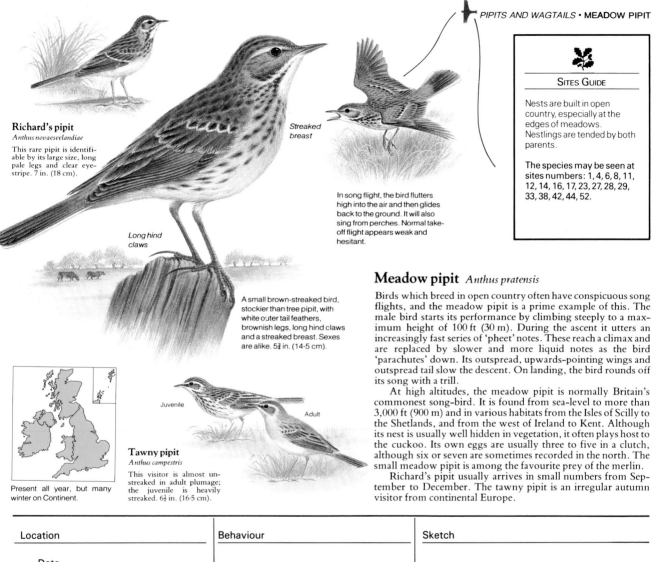

Richard's pipit
Anthus novaeseelandiae

This rare pipit is identifiable by its large size, long pale legs and clear eyestripe. 7 in. (18 cm).

Long hind claws

Streaked breast

In song flight, the bird flutters high into the air and then glides back to the ground. It will also sing from perches. Normal take-off flight appears weak and hesitant.

A small brown-streaked bird, stockier than tree pipit, with white outer tail feathers, brownish legs, long hind claws and a streaked breast. Sexes are alike. 5¾ in. (14·5 cm).

Present all year, but many winter on Continent.

Juvenile

Adult

Tawny pipit
Anthus campestris

This visitor is almost unstreaked in adult plumage; the juvenile is heavily streaked. 6½ in. (16·5 cm).

SITES GUIDE

Nests are built in open country, especially at the edges of meadows. Nestlings are tended by both parents.

The species may be seen at sites numbers: 1, 4, 6, 8, 11, 12, 14, 16, 17, 23, 27, 28, 29, 33, 38, 42, 44, 52.

Meadow pipit *Anthus pratensis*

Birds which breed in open country often have conspicuous song flights, and the meadow pipit is a prime example of this. The male bird starts its performance by climbing steeply to a maximum height of 100 ft (30 m). During the ascent it utters an increasingly fast series of 'pheet' notes. These reach a climax and are replaced by slower and more liquid notes as the bird 'parachutes' down. Its outspread, upwards-pointing wings and outspread tail slow the descent. On landing, the bird rounds off its song with a trill.

At high altitudes, the meadow pipit is normally Britain's commonest song-bird. It is found from sea-level to more than 3,000 ft (900 m) and in various habitats from the Isles of Scilly to the Shetlands, and from the west of Ireland to Kent. Although its nest is usually well hidden in vegetation, it often plays host to the cuckoo. Its own eggs are usually three to five in a clutch, although six or seven are sometimes recorded in the north. The small meadow pipit is among the favourite prey of the merlin.

Richard's pipit usually arrives in small numbers from September to December. The tawny pipit is an irregular autumn visitor from continental Europe.

Location	Behaviour	Sketch
Date		
Time		
Weather	Field marks	
Call		

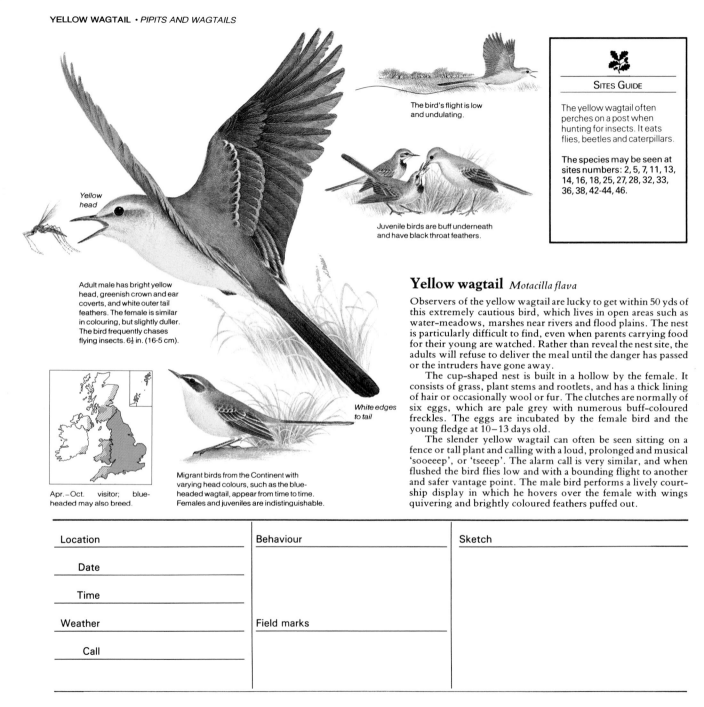

The bird's flight is low and undulating.

Juvenile birds are buff underneath and have black throat feathers.

Yellow head

Adult male has bright yellow head, greenish crown and ear coverts, and white outer tail feathers. The female is similar in colouring, but slightly duller. The bird frequently chases flying insects. 6½ in. (16·5 cm).

Apr.–Oct. visitor; blue-headed may also breed.

Migrant birds from the Continent with varying head colours, such as the blue-headed wagtail, appear from time to time. Females and juveniles are indistinguishable.

White edges to tail

Sites Guide

The yellow wagtail often perches on a post when hunting for insects. It eats flies, beetles and caterpillars.

The species may be seen at sites numbers: 2, 5, 7, 11, 13, 14, 16, 18, 25, 27, 28, 32, 33, 36, 38, 42-44, 46.

Yellow wagtail *Motacilla flava*

Observers of the yellow wagtail are lucky to get within 50 yds of this extremely cautious bird, which lives in open areas such as water-meadows, marshes near rivers and flood plains. The nest is particularly difficult to find, even when parents carrying food for their young are watched. Rather than reveal the nest site, the adults will refuse to deliver the meal until the danger has passed or the intruders have gone away.

The cup-shaped nest is built in a hollow by the female. It consists of grass, plant stems and rootlets, and has a thick lining of hair or occasionally wool or fur. The clutches are normally of six eggs, which are pale grey with numerous buff-coloured freckles. The eggs are incubated by the female bird and the young fledge at 10–13 days old.

The slender yellow wagtail can often be seen sitting on a fence or tall plant and calling with a loud, prolonged and musical 'sooeeep', or 'tseeep'. The alarm call is very similar, and when flushed the bird flies low and with a bounding flight to another and safer vantage point. The male bird performs a lively court-ship display in which he hovers over the female with wings quivering and brightly coloured feathers puffed out.

Location	Behaviour	Sketch
Date		
Time		
Weather	Field marks	
Call		

Juvenile bird, here fed by adult female, is brownish-grey above, dusty below, with black, crescent-shaped breast-band.

Cap and bib in one

Long tail

Adult's black and white plumage, including merged black cap and bib, and constant wagging of long tail are all distinctive features. Sexes are alike. 7 in. (18 cm).

Present all year; some birds migrate to Europe in winter.

Flight is heavily undulating, and accompanied constantly by the 'tschizzuck' flight call.

The European race, which may be seen on migration, has greyer upper parts and no join between cap and bib.

The pied wagtail often nests around farm buildings. Nest is built by female only.

SITES GUIDE

Rivers and lakes provide a frequent background for the pied wagtail, which often nests by shallow streams.

The species may be seen at sites numbers: 1, 3, 6, 7, 11-14, 16, 18, 19, 22, 23, 25-30, 33, 36-38, 42-44.

Pied wagtail *Motacilla alba yarrellii*

In many parts of Britain the pied wagtail is called the water wagtail, for it is often seen near ponds, streams and reservoirs. But just as frequently it is found in open country, particularly in the vicinity of stables, farmyards and cultivated areas. These provide the bird with a plentiful supply of the flies and other insects that make up most of its diet, and suitable nest sites in the form of holes in buildings and walls. Cavities in cliffs, stream banks and trees, and even abandoned cars also furnish acceptable nooks and crannies.

In courtship, two or more males chase a female in an undulating, dancing flight. The nest is an accumulation of twigs and other plant stems, grass, roots, dead leaves and moss, with a lining of hair, wool and feathers. In it is laid a clutch of five or six pale greyish-white or bluish-white eggs, uniformly sprinkled with greyish speckles. The chicks are fed by both parents. A pied wagtail with a beakful of insects is usually a reliable clue to the whereabouts of a nest.

Once regarded as a species in its own right, the pied wagtail is now regarded by ornithologists as a race of the white wagtail of mainland Europe and Asia.

Location	Behaviour	Sketch
Date		
Time		
Weather	Field marks	
Call		

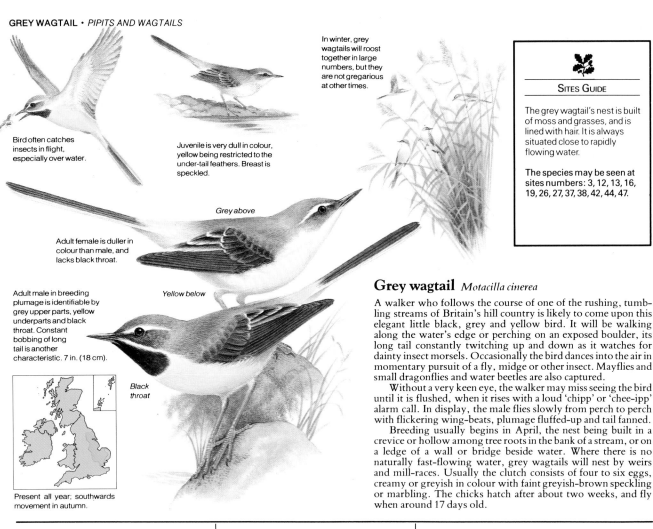

Bird often catches insects in flight, especially over water.

Juvenile is very dull in colour, yellow being restricted to the under-tail feathers. Breast is speckled.

In winter, grey wagtails will roost together in large numbers, but they are not gregarious at other times.

Grey above

Adult female is duller in colour than male, and lacks black throat.

Yellow below

Adult male in breeding plumage is identifiable by grey upper parts, yellow underparts and black throat. Constant bobbing of long tail is another characteristic. 7 in. (18 cm).

Black throat

Present all year; southwards movement in autumn.

SITES GUIDE

The grey wagtail's nest is built of moss and grasses, and is lined with hair. It is always situated close to rapidly flowing water.

The species may be seen at sites numbers: 3, 12, 13, 16, 19, 26, 27, 37, 38, 42, 44, 47.

Grey wagtail *Motacilla cinerea*

A walker who follows the course of one of the rushing, tumbling streams of Britain's hill country is likely to come upon this elegant little black, grey and yellow bird. It will be walking along the water's edge or perching on an exposed boulder, its long tail constantly twitching up and down as it watches for dainty insect morsels. Occasionally the bird dances into the air in momentary pursuit of a fly, midge or other insect. Mayflies and small dragonflies and water beetles are also captured.

Without a very keen eye, the walker may miss seeing the bird until it is flushed, when it rises with a loud 'chipp' or 'chee-ipp' alarm call. In display, the male flies slowly from perch to perch with flickering wing-beats, plumage fluffed-up and tail fanned.

Breeding usually begins in April, the nest being built in a crevice or hollow among tree roots in the bank of a stream, or on a ledge of a wall or bridge beside water. Where there is no naturally fast-flowing water, grey wagtails will nest by weirs and mill-races. Usually the clutch consists of four to six eggs, creamy or greyish in colour with faint greyish-brown speckling or marbling. The chicks hatch after about two weeks, and fly when around 17 days old.

Location	Behaviour	Sketch
Date		
Time		
Weather	Field marks	
Call		

Grey crown

Black face-stripe

Juvenile birds are generally similar to females, but their plumage is more scalloped.

Adult male can be recognised by its erect posture, grey crown and chestnut back and black face-stripe. 6¾ in. (17 cm).

Adult male in flight shows pointed wings and white outer tail feathers. Its flight is gently undulating.

Adult female is dull brown above and scalloped buff-brown below.

A bird sometimes impales its surplus food, such as insects, lizards and young birds, on thorns or barbed wire to be eaten later.

May–Sept. visitor; scarce, and decreasing in numbers.

Sites Guide

The nest of the red-backed shrike is made of grass stalks and moss, and lined with hair and roots. It is usually sited in a thorny bush.

This species is vulnerable to public pressure at its breeding sites, and for this reason no specific geographical references are given.

Red-backed shrike *Lanius collurio*

The shrike has been nicknamed the 'butcher-bird', because of its habit of storing its animal prey in 'larders'. The bird has a hawk-like hunting technique, and perches on top of a bush, fence or telegraph wire, watching for the slightest movement from insects or small reptiles, mammals and birds. When the prey is sighted, the shrike swoops down and snatches it up – and may impale it on a thorn or spike, to be eaten later.

The red-backed shrike population has decreased drastically both in England and Wales and on the Continent in the last 130 years or so. In the 1850s the bird was found as far north as the borders of Lancashire and Cumberland. But by 1950 it was mainly confined to England, south-east of a line from the Wash to the Severn estuary. The last 30 years have seen a further decline, and the bird's last stronghold is in East Anglia. The main reasons for the loss have been scarcity of food due to colder, wetter summers, the destruction of the bird's habitat, and the harm done by egg collectors.

The birds usually have one brood a year, when five to six whitish eggs with dark markings are laid. The nestlings are fed by both parents and leave the nest after 12–16 days.

Location	Behaviour	Sketch
Date		
Time		
Weather	Field marks	
Call		

Face-patch

A bare face-patch distinguishes the rook from the carrion crow, and gives a long-billed appearance. Plumage is black with a purple gloss; thigh feathers are thick. Sexes are alike. 18 in. (45 cm).

In breeding season, adults carry food to young in a throat pouch.

Thigh feathers

Present all year; winter immigrants from Continent.

Young bird has no face-patch, but possesses baggy thigh feathers.

Rooks nest sociably in tall trees, often near farm buildings. Noisy, communal flight displays are common.

The bird has a sedate walk, and often follows farm ploughs picking up leather-jackets and other insects.

Rook *Corvus frugilegus*

Before the leaves are out in spring, rooks congregate in breeding colonies high up in tall trees, their nests standing out against the network of bare branches. This habit of breeding early in conspicuous 'rookeries' makes counting the species relatively easy. The British rook population has fallen recently, possibly because of the ploughing–up of permanent pasture in favour of temporary crops of grass and clover, where the soil does not harbour so many of the bird's favourite insect foods – leather-jackets and wireworms.

Even so, some rookeries may number several thousand pairs: at Hatton Castle near Aberdeen, more than 6,000 nests have been counted. In 1424 James I of Scotland decreed the extermination of the rooks in his kingdom, because of their practice of feeding on corn; but the damage done by the bird to crops may well be balanced by its liking for insect pests.

The rook's nest is a bulky cup of sticks consolidated with soil and lined with roots, leaves, moss or wool. The female builds the nest with materials brought by her mate. A clutch usually consists of three to five bluish-green eggs, with greenish-brown or blackish-green speckles.

Location	Behaviour	Sketch
Date		
Time		
Weather	Field marks	
Call		

Young birds lack the contrasting plumage of adults. They are grey-brown above, speckled white below.

Flight is direct and fast on whirring, short wings.

SITES GUIDE

The dipper's young are fed by both birds. The nest may be under a bridge or the overhang of a river bank, or behind a waterfall.

The species may be seen at sites numbers: 3, 19, 26, 42, 44.

Dippers often prefer swimming to flying.

Short tail

Often seen perched on a boulder in a stream, the adult dipper has dark upper parts, white throat and breast and a chestnut waistband. Short tail and constant bobbing habit make it unmistakable. Sexes are alike. 7 in. (18 cm).

Continental black-bellied form, without chestnut band, occasionally appears in winter.

Dipper *Cinclus cinclus*

In contrast to all other birds, the dipper seeks its food by walking underwater on shallow river beds and the bottoms of streams. With its head down in search of water insects, tadpoles and worms, it may forge its way against the current, kept on its feet, probably, by the force of water pressing down on its broad back. Before submerging, the dipper often perches on rocks in the middle of rushing, tumbling water and repeatedly bobs up and down. Its legs flex, its wings quiver, its white eyelids blink, and its sweet, warbling song – which it maintains for most of the year – can be heard above the noise of the water.

The dipper is a plump, wren-like bird, with a distinctive, snow-white breast. Because of its feeding habits, it is mostly found in the uplands of western, central and northern Britain, where there are fast-running streams.

The bird's low, rapid and direct flight usually follows the course of a river; and it often spends the entire year on the same stretch of water. Dippers can swim on or under water. The bulky, domed nest is built of moss, and the white eggs, usually five, are laid in late March. Nestlings hatch in 15–18 days and fly after about three weeks. They can swim even earlier.

Present all year; some continental birds in winter.

The dipper has the remarkable ability to walk underwater up the beds of fast-flowing streams in search of food; it also dives into water from the air.

Location	Behaviour	Sketch
Date		
Time		
Weather	Field marks	
Call		

The bird is usually seen only briefly in flight as it flits from one bush or tussock to another.

The bird's streaked upper parts and rounded tail are clearly visible at close quarters.

Apr.–Sept. visitor; wide but thin distribution.

Buff underparts

Long tail

Adult bird is brown with whitish-buff underparts and a long tail. A distinctive trilling song sometimes reveals the elusive bird's presence. Sexes are alike. 5 in. (12·5 cm).

The bird's long middle toe enables it to grasp two stems at once when moving among tangled vegetation.

When disturbed, the bird usually creeps away through the grass rather than taking wing.

SITES GUIDE

The nest of the grasshopper warbler is built from dead grass, leaves and sticks and lined with hair. It is usually well hidden in a large grass tussock.

The species may be seen at sites numbers: 6, 7, 11, 14, 15, 19, 28, 29, 34, 36, 38, 42, 43, 46, 47, 52, 55.

Grasshopper warbler *Locustella naevia*

A watcher could be forgiven for thinking that the high-pitched whirr that comes from an expanse of tangled grass, bushes and brambles is being produced by some tiny machine. In fact the source of the sound is probably the grasshopper warbler, so named because its song resembles the sound made by some grasshoppers. An attempt to catch sight of the songster, however, is likely to be defeated by its 'voice-throwing' as it turns its head from side to side, and by its shy skulking habits.

The species arrives from winter quarters in north and west Africa between late April and the third week of May. The concealed, cup-shaped nest, approached from one way only, contains usually six creamy eggs, each so thickly speckled with fine purplish-brown spots as to appear dark. Male and female both incubate the eggs, which hatch after two weeks. Nestlings spend 10–12 days in the nest, fed by both parents.

Appetising morsels for grasshopper warblers are small insects and beetles, or spiders and woodlice. The nestlings also receive such succulent items as green caterpillars and aphids. By early August some birds will be flying south again, and by the end of September nearly all will have gone.

Location	Behaviour	Sketch
Date		
Time		
Weather	Field marks	
Call		

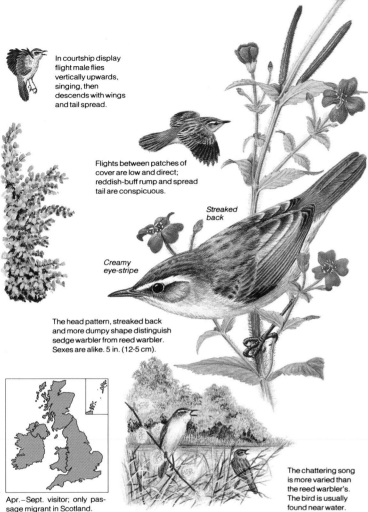

In courtship display flight male flies vertically upwards, singing, then descends with wings and tail spread.

Flights between patches of cover are low and direct; reddish-buff rump and spread tail are conspicuous.

Streaked back

Creamy eye-stripe

The head pattern, streaked back and more dumpy shape distinguish sedge warbler from reed warbler. Sexes are alike. 5 in. (12·5 cm).

Apr.–Sept. visitor; only passage migrant in Scotland.

The chattering song is more varied than the reed warbler's. The bird is usually found near water.

The bird spends much time skulking in cover to hunt for insects.

SITES GUIDE

The sedge warbler may sometimes be confused with the reed warbler, which is a slimmer and browner bird, but very difficult to spot.

The species may be seen at sites numbers: 1, 2, 7-11, 13-15, 18, 28, 29, 34, 36, 38, 40, 42-44, 46, 48, 51, 52, 54, 55.

Sedge warbler *Acrocephalus schoenobaenus*

One of many species that have benefited from the increase in young forestry plantations is the sedge warbler. It adapts well to their dense, rank vegetation, although it is traditionally a bird of damper areas such as osiers or reed-beds; it also occurs sometimes in standing crops.

Its attractive song, occasionally performed at night, is similar to the reed warbler's but more varied – a continuous and hurried series of notes, some chattering, some musical, each variant usually being repeated several times. Its own song is interspersed with accurate mimicry of other birds' songs.

Although more widespread than the reed warbler, this elusive bird is hard to spot, as it hides itself in low vegetation, hunting insects; and when it does emerge it darts straight to the next patch of cover. But its identity will be revealed by even a brief glimpse. Its colour is creamier than the reed warbler's, with bold streaks of darker colour on the back and wings and a prominent, creamy stripe above each eye. Usually five or six eggs are laid in a nest hidden low down in dense vegetation. The young, which hatch after about two weeks, are fed on small insects such as crane-flies, midges, beetles and dragonflies.

Location	Behaviour	Sketch
Date		
Time		
Weather	Field marks	
Call		

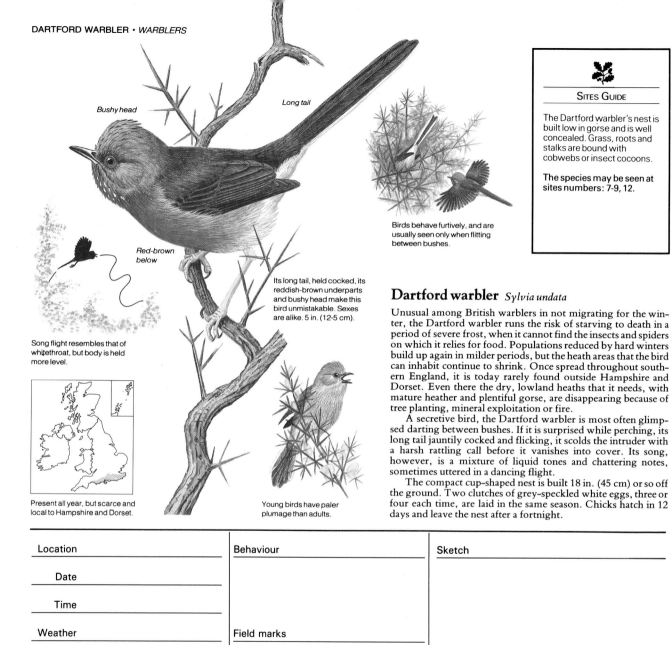

Bushy head

Long tail

Red-brown below

Song flight resembles that of whitethroat, but body is held more level.

Present all year, but scarce and local to Hampshire and Dorset.

Its long tail, held cocked, its reddish-brown underparts and bushy head make this bird unmistakable. Sexes are alike. 5 in. (12·5 cm).

Birds behave furtively, and are usually seen only when flitting between bushes.

Young birds have paler plumage than adults.

Dartford warbler *Sylvia undata*

Unusual among British warblers in not migrating for the winter, the Dartford warbler runs the risk of starving to death in a period of severe frost, when it cannot find the insects and spiders on which it relies for food. Populations reduced by hard winters build up again in milder periods, but the heath areas that the bird can inhabit continue to shrink. Once spread throughout southern England, it is today rarely found outside Hampshire and Dorset. Even there the dry, lowland heaths that it needs, with mature heather and plentiful gorse, are disappearing because of tree planting, mineral exploitation or fire.

A secretive bird, the Dartford warbler is most often glimpsed darting between bushes. If it is surprised while perching, its long tail jauntily cocked and flicking, it scolds the intruder with a harsh rattling call before it vanishes into cover. Its song, however, is a mixture of liquid tones and chattering notes, sometimes uttered in a dancing flight.

The compact cup–shaped nest is built 18 in. (45 cm) or so off the ground. Two clutches of grey-speckled white eggs, three or four each time, are laid in the same season. Chicks hatch in 12 days and leave the nest after a fortnight.

Location	Behaviour	Sketch
Date		
Time		
Weather	Field marks	
Call		

The lesser whitethroat sometimes sings while flying.

The nest is neat but frail. Sometimes the eggs can be seen from beneath.

Dark cheek

Brown wings

The short, rattling song is often heard from the shelter of a bush or thicket.

The bird lacks the red-brown colour of the whitethroat and is shorter-tailed, with dark cheeks. Sexes are alike. 5¼ in. (13·5 cm).

Cobwebs may be collected to festoon the rim of the nest.

Apr.–Sept. visitor; occasionally nests in Scotland.

The bird is less obtrusive than the whitethroat, with less jaunty movements.

Lesser whitethroat *Sylvia curruca*

Only by the narrow margin of a quarter of an inch is this bird 'lesser' than the common whitethroat, measuring up to 5¼ in. (13·5 cm) compared with the common whitethroat's 5½ in. (14 cm). At times the two species may share habitats, but the lesser whitethroat prefers areas with taller trees and shrubs, such as gardens and shrubberies, and avoids areas of sparse bushes. It is most easily distinguished by its brown wings, which lack the reddish tinge of the whitethroat's wings.

The bird's song often begins with an animated and attractive warble, then continues with a rattling note rapidly repeated five or six times, audible far away. Attempts to approach are usually thwarted by the bird's habit of moving long distances between snatches of song.

The nest, concealed amid thick vegetation, is a cup of dead grass and rootlets. When the young first leave the nest the parents proclaim anxiety for their brood's safety with a loud and persistent 'tac-tac-tac' and a distinctive trilling call. Wintering mainly in East Africa, just north of the Equator, the lesser whitethroat escaped the fate of so many common whitethroats during the Sahara drought of 1968–9.

Location	Behaviour	Sketch
Date		
Time		
Weather	Field marks	
Call		

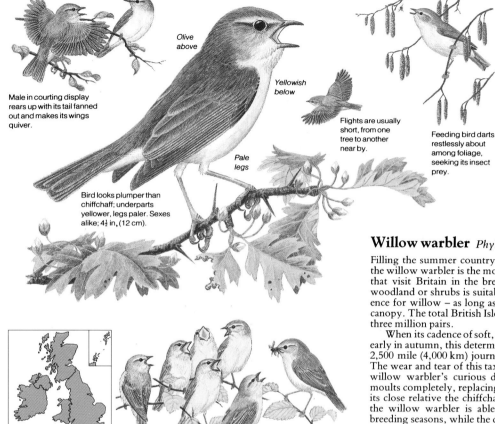

Male in courting display rears up with its tail fanned out and makes its wings quiver.

Olive above

Yellowish below

Flights are usually short, from one tree to another near by.

Feeding bird darts restlessly about among foliage, seeking its insect prey.

Pale legs

Bird looks plumper than chiffchaff; underparts yellower, legs paler. Sexes alike; 4½ in, (12 cm).

Apr.–Sept. visitor, breeding in wood and shrubland.

Young birds have much stronger yellow tinge than adult.

SITES GUIDE

The willow warbler usually builds its domed, feather-lined nest of moss and grass on the ground.

The species may be seen at sites numbers: 1-3, 6-9, 11-13, 16, 17, 19, 21-24, 26-28, 30, 33, 36-39, 41, 42, 44, 48, 51, 52, 54, 55.

Willow warbler *Phylloscopus trochilus*

Filling the summer countryside with its sweetly wistful song, the willow warbler is the most widely distributed of all the birds that visit Britain in the breeding season. Almost any area of woodland or shrubs is suitable – the bird has no special preference for willow – as long as the foliage does not form a closed canopy. The total British Isles population is probably more than three million pairs.

When its cadence of soft, liquid notes can no longer be heard, early in autumn, this determined little bird has started its annual 2,500 mile (4,000 km) journey to tropical and southern Africa. The wear and tear of this taxing migration may account for the willow warbler's curious distinction among British birds: it moults completely, replacing all its plumage, twice a year. Even its close relative the chiffchaff moults only once. Nevertheless the willow warbler is able to produce two broods in most breeding seasons, while the chiffchaff manages only one.

The domed nest with its side opening usually contains six eggs, white with pinkish or reddish-brown speckles. The hen alone incubates them, taking about 13 days, but the male helps in feeding the chicks during the 13 days they spend in the nest.

Location	Behaviour	Sketch
Date		
Time		
Weather	Field marks	
Call		

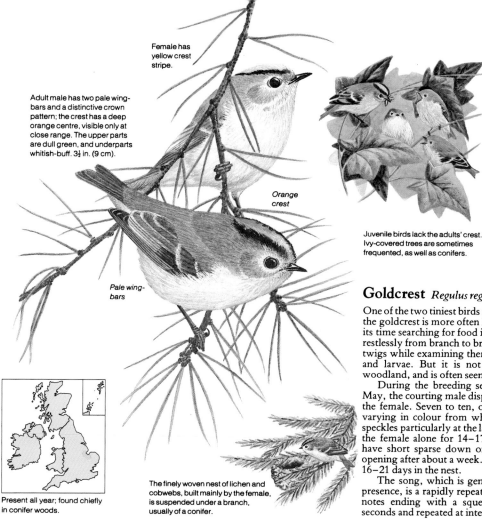

Female has yellow crest stripe.

Adult male has two pale wing-bars and a distinctive crown pattern; the crest has a deep orange centre, visible only at close range. The upper parts are dull green, and underparts whitish-buff. 3½ in. (9 cm).

Orange crest

Pale wing-bars

Juvenile birds lack the adults' crest. Ivy-covered trees are sometimes frequented, as well as conifers.

Present all year; found chiefly in conifer woods.

The finely woven nest of lichen and cobwebs, built mainly by the female, is suspended under a branch, usually of a conifer.

Sites Guide

Goldcrests are tame birds, often allowing very close approach. Together with the firecrest, they are Europe's smallest birds.

The species may be seen at sites numbers: 2, 3, 6, 11-14, 16, 19, 22, 24-27, 29, 30, 37, 38, 42, 44, 54.

Goldcrest *Regulus regulus*

One of the two tiniest birds in Europe – the other is the firecrest – the goldcrest is more often heard than seen, as it spends most of its time searching for food in the tops of coniferous trees. It flits restlessly from branch to branch, often clinging upside-down to twigs while examining them for spiders, insects, and their eggs and larvae. But it is not entirely dependent on coniferous woodland, and is often seen elsewhere.

During the breeding season, which starts in late April or May, the courting male displays his orange-and-yellow crest to the female. Seven to ten, occasionally up to 13, eggs are laid, varying in colour from white to buff, with purple or brown speckles particularly at the larger end. The eggs are incubated by the female alone for 14–17 days. The hatched chicks, which have short sparse down on their heads, are blind, their eyes opening after about a week. Both parents feed them during their 16–21 days in the nest.

The song, which is generally the first hint of a goldcrest's presence, is a rapidly repeated series of extremely high-pitched notes ending with a squeaky twitter, lasting three or four seconds and repeated at intervals.

Location	Behaviour	Sketch
Date		
Time		
Weather	Field marks	
Call		

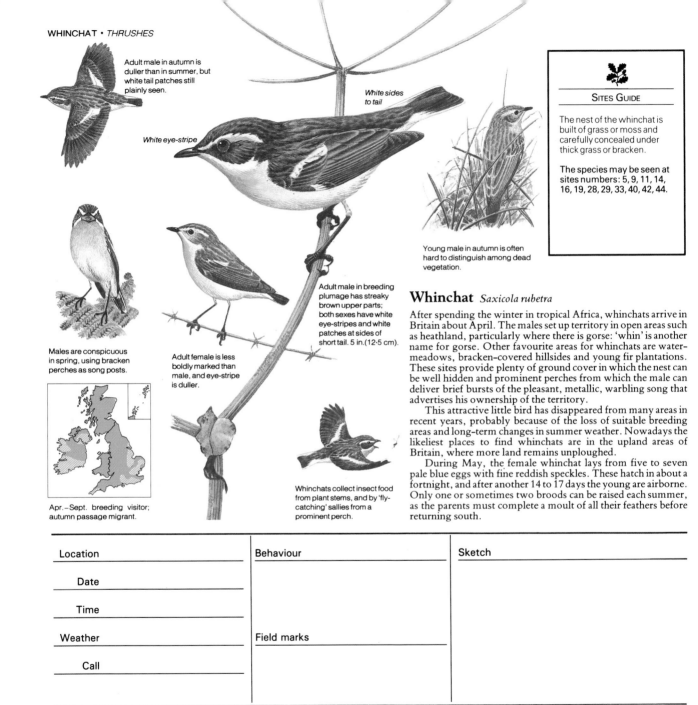

Adult male in autumn is duller than in summer, but white tail patches still plainly seen.

White sides to tail

White eye-stripe

Males are conspicuous in spring, using bracken perches as song posts.

Adult female is less boldly marked than male, and eye-stripe is duller.

Adult male in breeding plumage has streaky brown upper parts; both sexes have white eye-stripes and white patches at sides of short tail. 5 in.(12·5 cm).

Apr.–Sept. breeding visitor; autumn passage migrant.

Whinchats collect insect food from plant stems, and by 'fly-catching' sallies from a prominent perch.

Young male in autumn is often hard to distinguish among dead vegetation.

Whinchat *Saxicola rubetra*

After spending the winter in tropical Africa, whinchats arrive in Britain about April. The males set up territory in open areas such as heathland, particularly where there is gorse: 'whin' is another name for gorse. Other favourite areas for whinchats are water-meadows, bracken-covered hillsides and young fir plantations. These sites provide plenty of ground cover in which the nest can be well hidden and prominent perches from which the male can deliver brief bursts of the pleasant, metallic, warbling song that advertises his ownership of the territory.

This attractive little bird has disappeared from many areas in recent years, probably because of the loss of suitable breeding areas and long-term changes in summer weather. Nowadays the likeliest places to find whinchats are in the upland areas of Britain, where more land remains unploughed.

During May, the female whinchat lays from five to seven pale blue eggs with fine reddish speckles. These hatch in about a fortnight, and after another 14 to 17 days the young are airborne. Only one or sometimes two broods can be raised each summer, as the parents must complete a moult of all their feathers before returning south.

Location	Behaviour	Sketch
Date		
Time		
Weather	Field marks	
Call		

During courtship, males make erratic up-and-down twittering song flights.

Black head

White patch on neck

Chestnut breast

Adult female has fewer colour contrasts than male, with streaky upper parts and no white on rump. Adult male in winter is similar to female.

Young birds in autumn are pale, resembling whinchats but without bold eye-stripes.

Male in flight is distinguished from whinchat by lack of white tail markings.

Present all year, but breeding range has decreased.

Adult male in breeding plumage has black head, white patches on neck, wings and rump, and chestnut breast. Both sexes plump, with upright stance. 5 in. (12·5 cm).

Stonechats obtain insect food such as moths, spiders and flies mainly from the ground, where they sometimes perch.

SITES GUIDE

The stonechat's nest of moss, grass and hair is well hidden, low down in bushes or thick grass.

The species may be seen at sites numbers: 2, 4, 6, 8, 9, 12, 14, 16, 17, 33.

Stonechat *Saxicola torquata*

A call resembling the sound of two pebbles being banged together often betrays the presence of a stonechat – as well as explaining the origin of its name. Primarily a bird of gorse heathland, the stonechat is usually seen perching on a high vantage point, such as the top of a bush or telegraph wire; from there it scolds intruders with its 'wee-tac-tac' alarm. In Ireland and some parts of Britain stonechats can be found in moister areas.

Stonechats feed mainly on small creatures such as insects, worms and spiders, but they have been known to take small lizards, and they also eat some seeds. A male stonechat may be paired to more than one female, each of which lays five or six eggs, similar in appearance to those of the whinchat. The male helps to feed the young until they become independent.

Although the length of time from egg-laying to the flying of the young is about the same for stonechats as for whinchats, the stonechat frequently manages to raise three broods of young each year. This is because most stonechats stay in Britain all the year round and do not migrate south for the winter. As a result, many birds die during severe winters.

Location	Behaviour	Sketch
Date		
Time		
Weather	Field marks	
Call		

The wheatear often chases insects upwards in vertical flight, with fluttering wing-beats.

Adult female is brown with buff underparts, but has the same tail pattern as the male.

White rump

Grey above

Black cheeks

Adult male in summer has grey upper parts, black cheeks and wings, white rump and black, inverted-T tail pattern. In autumn he resembles the female. 6 in. (15 cm).

Juvenile bird is brown like adult female, but also heavily speckled.

Mar.–Oct. visitor, and also passage migrant.

In flight, white rump and black, T-shaped tail pattern are conspicuous.

When the wheatears arrive, usually in March, they can be seen seeking insects, larvae and centipedes in ploughed fields.

SITES GUIDE

Wheatears' nests are built under stones or in crevices. Both parents feed the dark grey nestlings with insects.

The species may be seen at sites numbers: 1, 12-14, 16, 33, 40, 42, 44.

Wheatear *Oenanthe oenanthe*

One of the first signs that spring is on its way is the arrival in Britain of the wheatear, among the earliest of the summer migrants. Normally, early arrivals from Africa are seen in southern England about the second week in March; most birds appear between the last week of March and mid-April.

The most noticeable feature of the wheatear is its white rump, visible as the bird flits low over the ground to perch on a prominent stone, clod of earth or other vantage point. The bird's common name comes from *hwit* and *oers*, Anglo-Saxon words for 'white' and 'rump'.

The wheatear is mainly a bird of upland Britain, and elsewhere occurs mostly on heathlands and coasts. It is in such areas that suitable nest sites in the form of holes in drystone walls or under large stones are most plentiful. The nest of loose grass, stems and leaves is built largely by the female. The four to seven pale blue eggs are laid in late March, or as late as June in the north. They hatch after 14 days and the young spend about two weeks in the nest. The wheatear is noted for its distinctive 'wee-chat-chat' call; its song is a vigorous, though brief, warble, intermingled with harsh rattlings and squeaky notes.

Location	Behaviour	Sketch
Date		
Time		
Weather	Field marks	
Call		

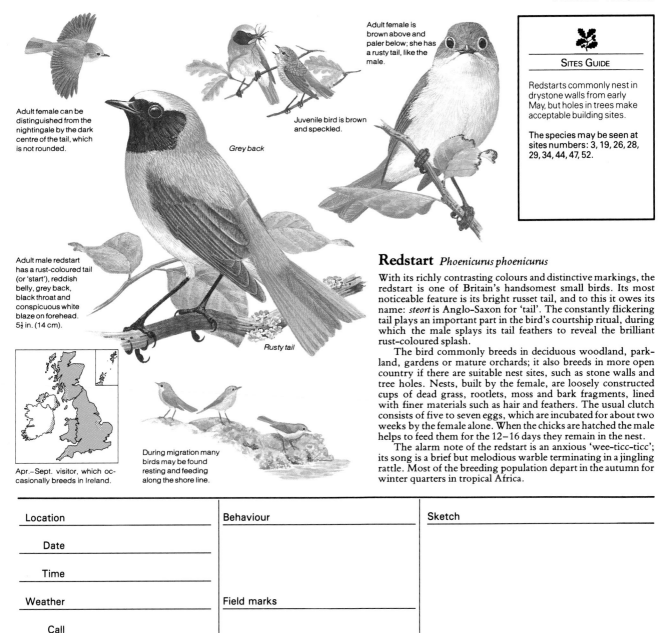

Adult female can be distinguished from the nightingale by the dark centre of the tail, which is not rounded.

Grey back

Adult female is brown above and paler below; she has a rusty tail, like the male.

Juvenile bird is brown and speckled.

Adult male redstart has a rust-coloured tail (or 'start'), reddish belly, grey back, black throat and conspicuous white blaze on forehead. 5½ in. (14 cm).

Rusty tail

Apr.–Sept. visitor, which occasionally breeds in Ireland.

During migration many birds may be found resting and feeding along the shore line.

Redstart *Phoenicurus phoenicurus*

With its richly contrasting colours and distinctive markings, the redstart is one of Britain's handsomest small birds. Its most noticeable feature is its bright russet tail, and to this it owes its name: *steort* is Anglo-Saxon for 'tail'. The constantly flickering tail plays an important part in the bird's courtship ritual, during which the male splays its tail feathers to reveal the brilliant rust-coloured splash.

The bird commonly breeds in deciduous woodland, parkland, gardens or mature orchards; it also breeds in more open country if there are suitable nest sites, such as stone walls and tree holes. Nests, built by the female, are loosely constructed cups of dead grass, rootlets, moss and bark fragments, lined with finer materials such as hair and feathers. The usual clutch consists of five to seven eggs, which are incubated for about two weeks by the female alone. When the chicks are hatched the male helps to feed them for the 12–16 days they remain in the nest.

The alarm note of the redstart is an anxious 'wee-ticc-ticc'; its song is a brief but melodious warble terminating in a jingling rattle. Most of the breeding population depart in the autumn for winter quarters in tropical Africa.

Location	Behaviour	Sketch
Date		
Time		
Weather	Field marks	
Call		

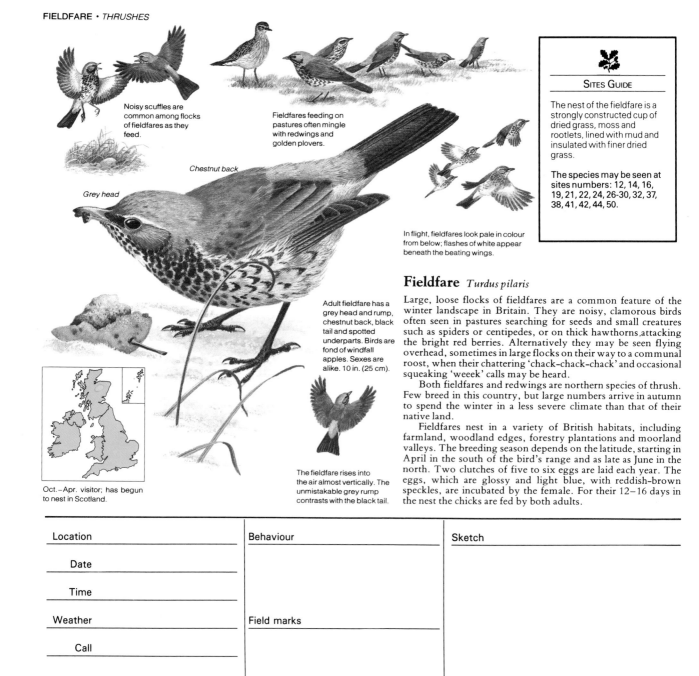

Noisy scuffles are common among flocks of fieldfares as they feed.

Fieldfares feeding on pastures often mingle with redwings and golden plovers.

Chestnut back

Grey head

In flight, fieldfares look pale in colour from below; flashes of white appear beneath the beating wings.

Adult fieldfare has a grey head and rump, chestnut back, black tail and spotted underparts. Birds are fond of windfall apples. Sexes are alike. 10 in. (25 cm).

Oct.–Apr. visitor; has begun to nest in Scotland.

The fieldfare rises into the air almost vertically. The unmistakable grey rump contrasts with the black tail.

SITES GUIDE

The nest of the fieldfare is a strongly constructed cup of dried grass, moss and rootlets, lined with mud and insulated with finer dried grass.

The species may be seen at sites numbers: 12, 14, 16, 19, 21, 22, 24, 26-30, 32, 37, 38, 41, 42, 44, 50.

Fieldfare *Turdus pilaris*

Large, loose flocks of fieldfares are a common feature of the winter landscape in Britain. They are noisy, clamorous birds often seen in pastures searching for seeds and small creatures such as spiders or centipedes, or on thick hawthorns, attacking the bright red berries. Alternatively they may be seen flying overhead, sometimes in large flocks on their way to a communal roost, when their chattering 'chack-chack-chack' and occasional squeaking 'weeek' calls may be heard.

Both fieldfares and redwings are northern species of thrush. Few breed in this country, but large numbers arrive in autumn to spend the winter in a less severe climate than that of their native land.

Fieldfares nest in a variety of British habitats, including farmland, woodland edges, forestry plantations and moorland valleys. The breeding season depends on the latitude, starting in April in the south of the bird's range and as late as June in the north. Two clutches of five to six eggs are laid each year. The eggs, which are glossy and light blue, with reddish-brown speckles, are incubated by the female. For their 12–16 days in the nest the chicks are fed by both adults.

Location	Behaviour	Sketch
Date		
Time		
Weather	Field marks	
Call		

Juvenile bird's tail colouring and paler underparts distinguish it from a young robin.

Chestnut tail is conspicuous on rare glimpse of nightingale in flight.

Chestnut tail

A chestnut tail is the only eye-catching feature of the adult bird, which is like an oversized robin in build and attitude. Seldom seen, it is usually identified by its song. Sexes are alike. 6½ in. (16·5 cm).

Apr.–Aug. visitor; rare outside breeding range.

A feeding bird may dart out of hiding to find insects.

The characteristic tail colour is usually all that is seen as the bird dives for cover.

SITES GUIDE

The nightingale's nest, of dead leaves lined with grass and hair, is often hidden in brambles or nettles, on or close to the ground.

The species may be seen at sites numbers: 5, 19, 28, 30, 34.

Nightingale *Luscinia megarhynchos*

Generations of poets have been inspired by the song of the nightingale. Milton, for instance, wrote of the 'nightingale, that on yon bloomy spray Warbl'st at eve, when all the woods are still'. The song, sometimes but not always delivered at dead of night, is remarkable for its tonal richness, variety and volume. It consists of a series of short phrases and single notes, usually repeated, often with increasing volume, some notes having a flute-like quality, others a more piping tone. The song period is short, lasting only from mid to late April until June.

The nightingale is a shy bird, generally to be found in open deciduous woodland where plenty of cover is provided by dense undergrowth of bramble, or by thickets of thorn bushes such as blackthorn. However, because the nightingale feeds largely on ground-living insects such as beetles, any site which has become too overgrown is deserted.

The four or five eggs laid in May are olive-green or olive-brown. Incubation takes about two weeks and is by the female alone. The young are fed for about 12 days by both parents. By the end of July many birds have started their journey back to Africa; and the stragglers have gone by the end of September.

Location	Behaviour	Sketch
Date		
Time		
Weather	Field marks	
Call		

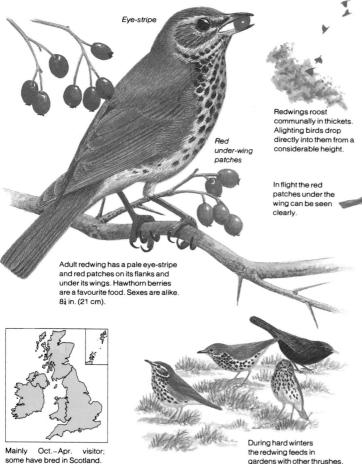

Eye-stripe

Red
under-wing
patches

Adult redwing has a pale eye-stripe
and red patches on its flanks and
under its wings. Hawthorn berries
are a favourite food. Sexes are alike.
8¼ in. (21 cm).

Mainly Oct.–Apr. visitor;
some have bred in Scotland.

Redwings roost
communally in thickets.
Alighting birds drop
directly into them from a
considerable height.

In flight the red
patches under the
wing can be seen
clearly.

Rhododendrons are
a favourite home for
pairs nesting in
Scotland.

During hard winters
the redwing feeds in
gardens with other thrushes.

Sites Guide

Like the song thrush, the
redwing may be seen
'listening' while searching on
the ground for snails, worms
or insects.

The species may be seen at
sites numbers: 3, 12, 14, 16,
21, 22, 24, 26-30, 32, 37, 38,
41, 42, 44, 50.

Redwing *Turdus iliacus*

On clear, starry nights in September and October the careful
listener may detect a thin, hissing 'seeeeip'-like sound at intervals overhead. It is the sign that redwings are in flight, calling to
keep in contact with their fellows. They will have set out from
northern Europe, where they breed, some hours before. Some
will remain in Britain; others will continue further south. The
severe winters of their breeding grounds mean that they must
seek in warmer climes for their food – berries such as hawthorn,
yew, holly and mountain ash, and invertebrates like worms,
snails and spiders.

A few redwings breed in northern Scotland, in woodlands of
birch, alder or pine, in spinneys, valleys, gullies among mountains or even in gardens. The nest is usually in a tree, against the
trunk, or in a shrub; other nests may be in tree stumps or steep
banks. The female builds the nest – a firm cup of dried grass,
fine twigs and moss – between May and July.

The eggs are smooth and glossy, pale blue or greenish-blue
in colour with fine specklings of reddish-brown. Incubation
lasts for up to 15 days. The nestlings are fed by both parents for
about two weeks in the nest, and for some time after they fledge.

Location	Behaviour	Sketch
Date		
Time		
Weather	Field marks	
Call		

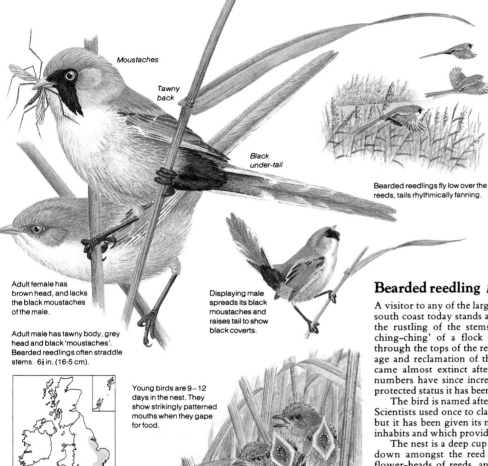

Moustaches

Tawny back

Black under-tail

Bearded reedlings fly low over the reeds, tails rhythmically fanning.

Adult female has brown head, and lacks the black moustaches of the male.

Adult male has tawny body, grey head and black 'moustaches'. Bearded reedlings often straddle stems. 6½ in. (16·5 cm).

Displaying male spreads its black moustaches and raises tail to show black coverts.

Young birds are 9–12 days in the nest. They show strikingly patterned mouths when they gape for food.

Present all year; has spread westwards from East Anglia.

Bearded reedling *Panurus biarmicus*

A visitor to any of the large reed beds in East Anglia or along the south coast today stands a reasonable chance of hearing, above the rustling of the stems, the far-carrying, bell-like 'ching-ching-ching' of a flock of bearded reedlings as they move through the tops of the reeds. Already threatened by the drainage and reclamation of the marshes, the bearded reedling became almost extinct after the severe winter of 1947; but its numbers have since increased, partly because of the specially protected status it has been given.

The bird is named after the black face markings of the male. Scientists used once to classify it as a member of the tit family, but it has been given its new name after the *Phragmites* reeds it inhabits and which provide its staple diet of seeds.

The nest is a deep cup of dead reeds and sedges, placed low down amongst the reed stems. It is lined with the feathery flower-heads of reeds, and occasionally some feathers. About six eggs are laid between April and July, the parents sharing all duties from nest-building onwards. Two broods are common. Family parties often remain together and group up with others after the breeding season.

Location	Behaviour	Sketch
Date		
Time		
Weather	Field marks	
Call		

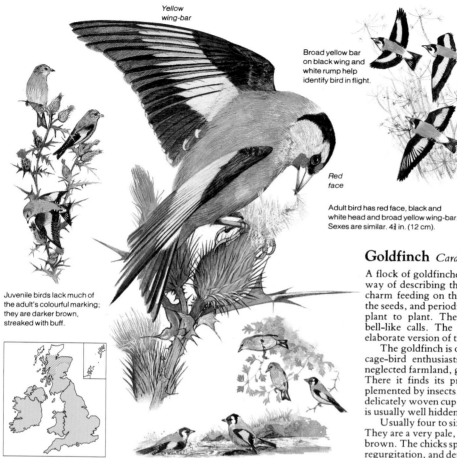

Yellow
wing-bar

Broad yellow bar
on black wing and
white rump help
identify bird in flight.

Red
face

Adult bird has red face, black and
white head and broad yellow wing-bar.
Sexes are similar. 4¾ in. (12 cm).

Juvenile birds lack much of
the adult's colourful marking;
they are darker brown,
streaked with buff.

Some birds stay all year;
others go south in winter.

Flocks are often seen bathing
together in summer.

Goldfinch *Carduelis carduelis*

A flock of goldfinches is called a 'charm', and there is no better
way of describing these delightful birds. It is a joy to watch a
charm feeding on thistles or groundsel, delicately picking out
the seeds, and periodically moving – with dancing flight – from
plant to plant. The pleasure is enhanced by their tinkling,
bell–like calls. The song is a pretty, liquid twittering – an
elaborate version of the flight notes.

The goldfinch is one of the most popular small birds among
cage-bird enthusiasts and birdwatchers alike. It is found in
neglected farmland, gardens and open areas with scattered trees.
There it finds its preferred diet of annual weed seeds, supplemented by insects. The nest, built by the female, is a neat and
delicately woven cup of plant material, including thistledown. It
is usually well hidden in the upper branches of small trees.

Usually four to six eggs are laid from late April to early May.
They are a very pale, bluish–white with a few streaks of reddish-
brown. The chicks spend about two weeks in the nest, are fed by
regurgitation, and depend on their parents for about a week after
fledging. During that time they make a constant twitter of
contact calls with the adult birds.

Location	Behaviour	Sketch
Date		
Time		
Weather	Field marks	
Call		

Juvenile birds lack any red colouring and have yellower bills than adults.

Redpolls are often seen by ponds, where they like to drink and bathe.

Most birds stay all year; some migrate, others visit.

Adult male in summer plumage has red forehead, black chin and pink breast and rump. Adult female generally lacks pink breast and rump. 4½–6 in. (12–15 cm).

Red forehead

Black chin

Pink breast

Native bird

Northern visitor

Larger, paler redpolls from northern Europe and Greenland may visit Britain in winter.

In winter, males have less pink on breast and rump. Birds feed in flocks on alder and birch seeds, often mixing with siskins.

Redpolls eat tree and plant seeds. Both sexes have buff-coloured double wing-bars.

SITES GUIDE

Redpolls often nest in loose-knit colonies. Silver birch trees and gorse bushes are popular nesting sites.

The species may be seen at sites numbers: 9, 12, 14, 15, 27-30, 32, 33, 37, 38, 42-44, 47, 48, 52.

Redpoll *Acanthis flammea*

Conifers, alders and birches are the favourite habitat of the redpoll. The population has swelled markedly in the last 35 years with the increase in conifer planting, and often overflows from woodlands to hedgerows and gardens with suitable vegetation.

Usually, the first indication of the redpoll's presence is its distinctive flight call, a rattling, bell-like 'ching, ching, ching'. Like most finches, its flight is undulating. It also has an unusual display flight – a series of loops and circles with slow wing-beats and occasional glides – sometimes performed by several males together. The alarm call is a musical, plaintive 'tsooeet'.

Redpolls start to breed at the end of April in the south. Nesting sites vary from low bushes to high tree branches, and the nest is a small, rather untidy cup of twigs, dried grass and plant stems neatly lined with hair, thistledown and occasionally feathers. The four or five eggs are whitish-blue finely speckled with lilac and purple-brown, and the female incubates them for 10–13 days. Both parents tend the downy, dark grey nestlings for about a fortnight until they are fledged, and then for a short while afterwards. The redpoll's diet of seeds is sometimes supplemented by small insects and their larvae.

Location	Behaviour	Sketch
Date		
Time		
Weather	Field marks	
Call		

Red forehead

Chestnut back

Red breast

Male in flight. Both sexes show white-edged wing and tail feathers.

In late summer, some males develop a gold breast and forehead in place of red.

Male

Female

Female lacks red colouring and is more streaked. Linnets like bushy country and prefer low perches.

Adult male in summer has grey head, red forehead and breast, and chestnut back; but is grey in breeding season, and tail is forked. 5¼ in. (13·5 cm).

Most birds stay all year; some migrate in autumn.

In winter, large flocks search on the ground for weed seeds.

Sites Guide

The linnet's nest is usually built within a few feet of the ground. Gorse and bramble bushes are favourite sites.

The species may be seen at sites numbers: 4, 6, 8, 9, 11, 14, 16, 17, 19, 23, 26, 27, 29, 30, 33, 37, 42, 44.

Linnet *Acanthis cannabina*

Flax seeds were once considered to be the linnet's favourite food, so its name is a diminutive of *lin*, the Old English word for flax. It eats many other plant seeds, however. In the 19th century, linnets were once kept as cage birds because of their musical song, and this led to a decline in their population. Legal protection in the early part of this century brought about a recovery, but now the population is again reported to be declining, probably because the increased use of weed-killers has depleted the food supply.

Linnets breed from mid-April, often in small colonies. The female builds the nest, a rather ragged cup of plant stalks, grass and moss with a nest lining of hair and wool. She alone incubates the four to six bluish-white, purple-speckled eggs for 10–14 days. The male helps to feed the grey nestlings for their fortnight or so in the nest, the diet of seeds being well supplemented with small moths, caterpillars and other insects.

The linnet's twittering song is usually delivered from an exposed spray of a bush, sometimes by several males in chorus. It can be heard at any time from January to October, but most often between the end of March and late July.

Location	Behaviour	Sketch
Date		
Time		
Weather	Field marks	
Call		

Heavy head

Streaked plumage

During its display flight the male bird leaves its legs dangling.

SITES GUIDE

The corn bunting will nest among dense ground vegetation, but may also choose a higher site in a hedge.

The species may be seen at sites numbers: 14, 16, 29, 34, 37.

Little bunting
Emberiza pusilla

A small, rare migrant distinguished by its black-bordered chestnut crown and cheeks. It may be seen near water.

Adult bird's streaked brown plumage, large size and heavy-looking head and bill are the corn bunting's main distinctive features. Sexes are alike. 7 in. (18 cm).

Present all year; numbers declining in western Britain.

Corn buntings often feed around farm buildings in winter, in the company of other seed-eating birds such as the house sparrow.

Corn bunting *Emberiza calandra*

As well as being the largest of British buntings, the corn bunting is also the drabbest. It is a gregarious bird, often found in the company of other buntings outside the breeding season. As its name suggests, one of its favourite haunts is the cornfield, but it also frequents other open, lowland areas with few trees.

The song, a rapidly repeated note ending with a flourish and repeated regularly six to eight times a minute, is usually delivered from a hawthorn bush, fence post or telegraph wire. The male's display consists of a series of short upward flights, then hovering low, legs dangling, over the female on the ground before alighting.

The nest, a fairly loose cup of grasses and plant stems, lined with finer grasses, rootlets and animal hair, is usually built on the ground in grassy areas with thistles or other tall plants, or up to 5 ft (1·5 m) above the ground in a hedge. The eggs, usually three to five, are whitish with bold blackish-brown lines and spots. These are incubated for 12–13 days by the female, which also mainly feeds the hatched young; they spend about ten days in the nest. The diet consists mainly of fruits and seeds, supplemented by insects and a few molluscs and worms.

Location	Behaviour	Sketch
Date		
Time		
Weather	Field marks	
Call		

Bright yellow head

White tail feathers show up in flight. Its chestnut rump distinguishes the bird from the cirl bunting.

Females are duller in colour than males, and more streaked. Juveniles are very similar to females.

Present all year. Sedentary; widespread in open country.

Adult male has bright yellow head and breast, and sings lustily. Upper parts are chestnut streaked with black. 6¼ in. (16·5 cm).

Yellowhammers feed on the ground. In winter they are often seen feeding in flocks, in the company of finches and other buntings.

Yellow breast

SITES GUIDE

The yellowhammer's nest is built by the female, and is usually low down. Young birds spend about two weeks in the nest.

The species may be seen at sites numbers: 3, 4, 6, 8, 11-14, 16, 17, 19, 23-30, 33, 38, 42, 44, 54.

Yellowhammer *Emberiza citrinella*

Countrymen say that the yellowhammer's song is 'a-little-bit-of-bread-and-no-cheese'. It requires a little imagination to relate this phrase to the bird's simple repetition of a single note – 'chiz-iz-iz-iz-iz-iz-zeee' – or to any of the several variations.

Yellowhammers are common in areas of grassland, fields with hedgerows, allotments and commons – in fact almost any open area with low cover but few trees. Like other buntings they feed mainly on the ground, but perch on bushes and telegraph wires to deliver their song at intervals from February to the end of August. Breeding starts from the end of April; the courtship is a boisterous, madcap affair with the male hotly pursuing the female in a headlong, twisting flight that often ends with both birds tumbling through the branches in a flurry of feathers.

The nest, built by the female, is a neat cup of grasses, moss and plant stems lined with grass and hair. It is built on the ground in cover and concealed by overhanging plants, but occasionally it is built a few feet up in a thick bush. The three or four eggs are white or purplish-white with bold scribblings; these have given rise to the alternative name of 'scribble lark' for the bird in some country areas.

Location	Behaviour	Sketch
Date		
Time		
Weather	Field marks	
Call		

Pairs of reed buntings are often found in drier areas, but never far from water.

Black head and throat

Adult female lacks the all-black head of male, but has black and white moustache-like streaks. Underparts are white.

SITES GUIDE

The nest of the reed bunting is usually well hidden and built close to or on the ground. Reed-beds and sewage farms are popular sites.

The species may be seen at sites numbers: 1, 6-8, 12, 13, 16, 18, 25, 27-29, 36-38, 40, 43, 46, 48, 51.

White outer tail feathers

Male in winter lacks most of its black plumage. The male bird frequently flicks its wings and tail, or spreads its tail showing white outer feathers.

Adult male in summer has distinctive black head and throat with white, moustache-like streak and nape. The upper body is rich brown streaked with black. White outer tail feathers are conspicuous. 6 in. (15 cm).

Reed bunting *Emberiza schoeniclus*

With its white collar and moustachial streak and black head, the male reed bunting is reminiscent of a Victorian Guards officer. Clinging to a swaying reed, the bird delivers its chirruping song, a simple 'cheep–cheep–cheep–chizzup', with an occasional flick of the tail before flying jerkily to another clump of reeds.

The reed bunting is less appropriately named than it once was, for in recent years it has extended its range from the reed beds of fenland and river bank to drier places such as farm hedgerows, downland scrub and forestry plantations. In some areas it has been seen visiting gardens to feed along with house sparrows and greenfinches. Its favourite breeding grounds, however, are still the marshy places and riversides, where the female builds her nest in a tussock of rush or among dense vegetation close to the ground.

The nest is a cup of grass and moss lined with fine grasses, reed flowers and hair. A clutch usually numbers four or five eggs, brownish–olive or buff with a few streaks and spots of blackish–brown. The chicks hatch in two weeks and spend about two weeks in the nest, tended by both parents. Two, or occasionally three, broods may be raised each year.

Present all year; Continental birds on passage.

Reed buntings often associate with other birds such as yellowhammers in stubble fields while searching for winter food.

Location	Behaviour	Sketch
Date		
Time		
Weather	Field marks	
Call		

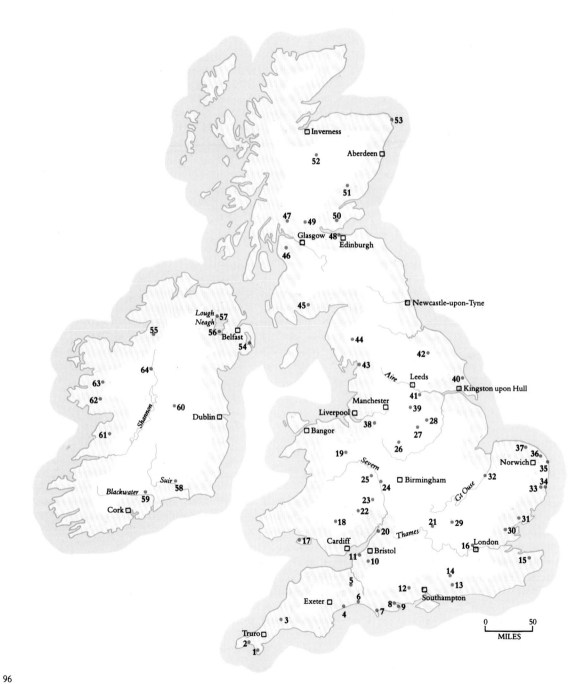

Inverness □
53 •
52 •
Aberdeen □
51 •
47 • 49 • 50 •
48 • Glasgow □
Edinburgh □
46 •
45 •
Newcastle-upon-Tyne □
Lough Neagh
57 •
56 •
Belfast □
54
55
44 •
42 •
43 •
64 •
Aire
Leeds •
40 •
□ Kingston upon Hull
63 •
41 •
62 •
Manchester •
39 •
60 •
Liverpool •
28 •
Dublin □
38 •
27 •
61 •
Shannon
26 •
37 • 36 •
19 •
Norwich □ 35 •
34 •
25 •
Severn
Birmingham □
32 •
33 •
24 •
Gt Ouse
58 •
23 •
Suir
22 •
31 •
59 •
21 •
29 •
30 •
Blackwater
18 •
Thames
Cork □
20 •
16 •
London □
17 •
Cardiff □
15 •
11
Bristol □
10 •
14 •
5 •
12 •
13 •
6 •
Exeter □
8 •
Southampton □
4 •
7 • 9 •
3 •
Truro □
2 •
1 •

0   50
MILES

96

The Sites

A descriptive gazetteer of places around Britain to see the birds on pages 12-95.

Order

The sites are featured in a special order, designed for ease of reference. They follow each other in a sequence determined by the Ordnance Survey's grid reference system, which works from west to east, and from south to north. The first sites described are those in Cornwall, in other words those furthest west and furthest south; the last sites described on mainland Britain are in north-east Scotland; Ulster and the Republic of Ireland are listed separately at the end.

For additional ease of reference, the sites are, however, grouped in regions and counties, and this framework takes precedence over the order required by the grid system; so that, for example, all the sites in Wales, from south to north, are listed together; then the list continues, starting afresh with the south-west corner of the Midlands, ie Gloucestershire.

Location of sites

Each site is described in terms of access from a nearby major road or town, or other major landmark. In England, Scotland and Wales, the number of the Ordnance Survey Landranger sheet (scale 1:50 000) on which the site occurs is also given, together with a grid reference number for exact and speedy location of the site on the map. Full directions on how to read a numerical grid reference are given on all Landranger sheets. Six-figure grid reference numbers are accurate to the nearest hundred metres and these are given where possible; however, it is sometimes more appropriate to quote a four-figure grid reference, accurate to the nearest kilometre, when a large area is in question. A quality motoring map will, in most cases, be adequate to locate a given site generally. The larger scale Landranger mapping is invaluable once you have arrived, for it shows public footpaths and details which enable the user to make the most of a given area.

Bird names in bold type

Bird names in **bold** are those which are featured in the identification section, pages 12-95.

Ornithological terms

A glossary explaining the meaning of ornithological terms is on pages 123-24.

1 The Loe
2 Marazion Marsh
3 Lanhydrock
4 Branscombe and Salcombe Regis
5 West Sedgemoor
6 Golden Cap Estate
7 Radipole Lake
8 Middlebere Heath and Hartland Moor
9 Studland and Godlingston Heath
10 Chew Valley
11 Failand
12 Bramshaw Commons
13 Petworth Park
14 Frensham Common
15 Stodmarsh
16 Osterley Park
17 Ryder's Down
18 Llangorse Lake
19 Erdigg
20 Slimbridge
21 Boarstall Duck Decoy
22 Breinton Springs

23 Brockhampton
24 Kinver Edge
25 Dudmaston
26 Dovedale
27 Hardwick Hall
28 Clumber Park
29 Ashridge
30 Danbury and Lingwood Commons
31 Abberton Reservoir
32 Ouse Washes
33 Dunwich Heath
34 Minsmere
35 Breydon Water
36 Horsey Mere
37 Blickling
38 Tatton Park
39 Worsbrough Mill and Country Park
40 Hornsea Mere
41 Fairburn Ings
42 Bransdale
   Lake District (box)
43 Leighton Moss

44 Hartsop and Caudale
45 Threave
46 Lochwinnoch
47 Loch Lomond
48 Duddingston Loch
49 Flanders Moss
50 Loch Leven
51 Loch of Kinnordy
52 Insh Marshes
53 Loch of Strathbeg
54 Castle Ward
55 Castlecaldwell
56 Lough Neagh
57 Lough Beg
58 Coolfin Marshes
59 Lismore Callows
60 Westmeath Lakes
61 Ballyallia Lake
62 Lough Corrib
63 Lough Carra
64 River Shannon

THE SOUTH WEST

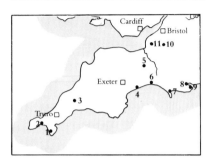

CORNWALL

1 The Loe

LOCATION **On the Lizard, 2 miles (3 km) south of Helston. Take A394 out of town, then B3304 to Porthleven, followed by track roads for one-and-a-half miles (2.5 km) east into Penrose Estate.** *Landranger Sheet 203, 645250.*

The Loe forms the central part of this south Cornwall estate in an Area of Outstanding Natural Beauty. Loe Pool, its most interesting feature, is the largest body of fresh water in Cornwall with an area of 150 acres and is separated from the sea by a broad shingle bar. The pool itself is a prime bird site and includes marshy willow carr at its northern end with regular aquatic breeding birds. Apart from this wetland, the estate includes coastal grassland, oakwood (lesser spotted woodpecker, garden warbler and blackcap), sand-cliffs with a **sand martin** colony, and shingle and sand foreshore (ringed plover and sanderling in winter).

Highlights

Loe Pool attracts a great diversity of overwintering wildfowl.

Time and season

Winter especially for ducks. The coastal section tends to get crowded with tourists in high summer. All year: **mallard, tufted duck, mute swan, coot, skylark, meadow pipit,** rock pipit, **pied wagtail, goldfinch, linnet.** Winter: **red-throated diver,** red-necked grebe, **teal, gadwall, wigeon, pintail, shoveler,** scaup, **pochard, goldeneye,** goosander. Summer: **swallow, sand martin, wheatear,** reed warbler, **sedge warbler, willow warbler,** chiffchaff, **reed bunting.**

2 Marazion Marsh

LOCATION **Two miles (3 km) east of Penzance and north of Mount's Bay. From Penzance follow the A30 eastwards and after 2 miles (3 km), fork right on to the A394 towards Marazion. A good vantage point is from the coast road after the railway bridge.** *Landranger Sheet 203, 510313.*

This exceptionally rich wetland site of marsh, pools and reed beds is actually the site of a submerged forest. There is a **heronry** in large pines to the north of the marsh and **herons** have been known to nest in the reeds themselves. The reed beds hold the most westerly population of reed warblers in the UK; the best view is from the roadbridge over the railway. Willow scrub to the east of the marsh holds

goldcrest and firecrest during autumn. Huge winter starling roost attracts sparrowhawk. Interesting spring migrants include Savi's warbler.

Highlights

Its strategic position at the extreme south-west of the country make it an excellent site for wader passage.

Time and season

Winter: **bittern,** Slavonian grebe (offshore), sparrowhawk, **water rail, snipe,** jack snipe. Spring: great northern diver (offshore), **garganey, shoveler, gadwall, ruff, yellow wagtail.** Summer: **heron, buzzard, stonechat, warblers.** Autumn: spotted crake, **greenshank,** wood sandpiper, **goldcrest,** firecrest.

3 Lanhydrock

LOCATION **Two-and-a-half miles (4 km) south of Bodmin, off the B3268.** *Landranger Sheet 200, 085636.*

This large estate situated on the western side of the River Fowey includes a mile-long stretch of the riverside, rich aquatic vegetation alternating with shingle banks. There are also three small tributary streams and a pond. The property also contains an interesting area of dwarf shrub heath, parkland with old oak trees, two main blocks of deciduous woodland and conifer plantations. Woodland species include sparrowhawk and pied flycatcher, the latter being a rare breeding species in Cornwall.

Although the estate is popular during

the summer months, few visitors venture further than the house and surrounding parkland. There is a car park at Respryn Bridge which gives access to the river.

Highlights
Kingfisher and **dipper** on the river and a variety of parkland birds.

Time and season
Spring and early summer for a wide variety of breeding birds. All year: **heron, kestrel, moorhen, kingfisher, rook, dipper, goldcrest, grey wagtail, yellowhammer.** Winter: **woodcock, redwing,** siskin. Summer: **swallow, redstart, willow warbler,** chiffchaff, spotted flycatcher, **pied wagtail.**

DEVON

4 Branscombe and Salcombe Regis

LOCATION **Two adjacent areas of east Devon coast and hinterland stretching 4 miles (6.5 km) from Branscombe Mouth to Dunscombe Cliff, south of Salcombe Regis. Access off the A3052 between Seaton and Sidmouth.** *Landranger Sheet 192, 210880–150880.*

One of the National Trust's richest properties for wildlife in the South West; it forms part of the Salcombe to Beer Coast Site of Special Scientific Interest (SSSI). The property is best known for its excellent range of grassland and scrub. Abundant thistles

make an excellent source of food for mixed flocks of finches during autumn and winter. Meadow, marsh, cliff and woodland add to the beauty and interest of this estate.

Highlights
The southerly and sheltered location provides refuge for migrant birds especially in the scrub and undercliff areas.

Time and season
All year: **buzzard, kestrel, rook, stonechat, meadow pipit, goldfinch, linnet, yellowhammer.** Summer: **swallow,** house martin, **lesser whitethroat, tree pipit.**

SOMERSET

5 West Sedgemoor

LOCATION **Remnant of the once extensive Somerset Levels, 6 miles (10 km) east of Taunton along the A358 then the A378. West Sedgemoor is bounded by the villages of Curry Rivel, Burrow Bridge, Durston and North Curry.** *Landranger Sheet 193, 365255.*

The RSPB Reserve at the centre of the moor consists of numerous rectangular fields of wet grassland intersected by water-filled ditches. The area is often flooded in winter, attracting a wide variety of waterfowl and waders.

At the southern edge of the moor is a steep ridge with deciduous woodland which has a **heronry,** breeding **buzzard** and **nightingale.**

Highlights
Up to 2,000 whimbrel in spring.

Time and season
Winter for dabbling ducks and **swans,** autumn for passage waders. All year: **heron, buzzard, redshank, curlew, snipe.** Winter: **wigeon, pintail, shoveler, tufted duck, pochard,** Bewick's swan, dunlin, golden plover, lapwing. Summer: **black-tailed godwit, yellow wagtail, whinchat, nightingale.**

DORSET

6 Golden Cap Estate

LOCATION **Three miles (5 km) south-west of Bridport, access via A35 from Morcombelake and Chideck, also footpaths from Lower Eype and Eype.** *Landranger Sheet 193, 400920.*

A beautiful estate of nearly 2,000 acres. The main part consists of a broad bowl of little valleys opening to the sea. Beyond the Cap the property stretches 5 miles (8 km) eastwards along the coast to Eype Mouth. The estate includes heath, scrub, grassland, flushes and streams, coastal landslips and several small pockets of woodland. Information centre just over 1 mile (1.5 km) along Stonebarrow Lane going east out of Charmouth.

Highlights
Spring birdsong – thrushes and **warblers** – and **buzzard** courtship display.

Time and season

All year: **mallard, buzzard, kestrel, partridge, lapwing, snipe, skylark, rook, stonechat, goldcrest, meadow pipit, pied wagtail, linnet, yellowhammer, reed bunting.** Summer: **cuckoo, swallow, grasshopper warbler, willow warbler,** chiffchaff, **lesser whitethroat, tree pipit.**

7 Radipole Lake

LOCATION **In the centre of Weymouth; access under railway bridge at north-west end of boat basin.** *Landranger Sheet 194, 676796.*

Radipole Lake, formed by the blocking off of the estuary of the River Wey, is an interesting RSPB Reserve of some 200 acres. The lake is part-bordered by reed-swamp with water meadows to the north. The paths at the southern end of the reserve are bordered by dense scrub of buddleia and bramble. This is a well-managed reserve with a rich bird life. An information centre caters for the needs of disabled visitors. As many as 236 species have been recorded.

Rarities include pied-bill grebe (US) corncrake and **Dartford warbler.**

Highlights

Breeding **bearded reedling** and Cetti's warbler, winter wildfowl; proximity to the coast brings interesting passage migrants such as little gull.

Time and season

Spectacular in late summer and early autumn as feeding station for large numbers of **sedge** and reed **warblers;** also large roosts of **yellow wagtails,** swallows and **martins.** All year: **great crested grebe, little grebe, heron, mallard, mute swan, kingfisher, reed bunting.** Winter: **teal, gadwall, pintail, shoveler, tufted duck, pochard, goldeneye, water rail, snipe, pied wagtail** (roost), **bearded reedling.** Summer: **grasshopper warbler,** reed warbler, **sedge warbler, willow warbler,** chiffchaff, **lesser whitethroat.** Passage: bar-tailed godwit, green sandpiper, wood sandpiper, **common sandpiper, redshank,** spotted redshank, **greenshank,** dunlin, **ruff.**

8 Middlebere Heath and Hartland Moor

LOCATION **Three miles (5 km) east of Wareham via the A351 to Stoborough, then left past Ridge towards Arne.** *Landranger Sheet 195, 940840 to 980870.*

A large and varied property that lies adjacent to the RSPB Reserve of Arne. This rich site includes wet and dry heath, mire and fen, reed beds, extensive areas of salt-marsh, pockets of scrub and some meadowland. The Hartland Moor section is a National Nature Reserve and is leased to the Nature Conservancy Council. The whole area is fascinating for its wildlife generally, including insects, amphibians and reptiles. A few bridleways and footpaths cross the property. The National Trust property of Corfe Castle and Common lies a few miles to the south and Studland Bay Estate a few miles to the east.

Highlights

Good area for listening to **sedge warbler** and **reed bunting** singing. **Dartford warbler** breeds periodically.

Time and season

Summer for heathland birds, autumn and winter for waders and wildfowl in and around Poole Harbour. All year: **mallard, teal,** shelduck, **water rail, moorhen, redshank, stonechat, meadow pipit, Dartford warbler, linnet, yellowhammer, reed bunting.** Winter: **great crested grebe, wigeon, goldeneye, hen harrier, curlew,** dunlin, oystercatcher. Summer: **cuckoo, nightjar, sedge warbler,** reed warbler, **willow warbler,** chiffchaff.

9 Studland and Godlingston Heath

LOCATION **Ten miles (16 km) east of Wareham. Follow the A351 towards Swanage, then turn left on to the B3351 to Studland, through the village towards the ferry, passing toll gate. Access from the north (Poole and Bournemouth) via the ferry at Sandbanks. Good car park facilities around Studland village and at South Haven Point.** *Landranger Sheet 195, 030480.*

A magnificent area of lowland heath forming part of the National Trust's Corfe Castle Estate and leased to the Nature Conservancy Council as a

National Nature Reserve. A focus of the reserve is a freshwater lagoon known as Little Sea. A hide at its northern end gives good views of waterfowl and waders during winter, and during the summer scrub woodland bordering the lagoon has breeding **warblers.** There is also meadowland, salt-marsh, fen, mud-flats, dune slacks and foreshore.

Common and Sandwich terns feed offshore during summer; sanderling turn up in Studland Bay in large numbers during autumn; shearwaters, gannets and skuas are often sighted on passage.

Highlights
Good chance of sightings of heathland birds especially **Dartford warbler, nightjar** song and display flights at twilight.

Time and season
Winter: Slavonian grebe, **teal, wigeon, tufted duck, pochard,** Brent goose, **water rail,** bar-tailed godwit. Summer: **nightjar, sedge warbler, reed warbler, Dartford warbler, willow warbler,** chiffchaff, **whinchat, stonechat, linnet, redpoll.**

10 Chew Valley Lake

LOCATION **About 7 miles (11 km) south of Bristol. Surrounding roads give adequate views: the A367 (Bath to Weston) on the south-eastern side between Bishop Sutton and West Harptree, and at Harptree the B3114 turns right past the western side of the lake to Chew Stoke. Another good vantage point is at Herriot's Bridge on the A368 on the southern** side of the lake. *Landranger Sheet 172, 560167.*

A man-made reservoir of over 1,200 acres, with natural banks and a large island in the north-eastern corner. The south side of the lake has extensive reed beds and shallows, with a public bird-watching hide south of Herriot's Bridge. Permits for access to the banks are available from Woodford Lodge, the Water Authority building on the western side of the lake.

Highlights
A prime site to watch water-birds at all seasons; impressive list of passage waders.

Time and season
Winter: **gadwall, wigeon, shoveler, pintail, pochard, goldeneye,** goosander, smew, **Bewick's swan, water rail, bearded reedling.** Summer: **garganey,** shelduck, reed warbler, **sedge warbler.** Passage: black-necked grebe, **gadwall,** little ringed plover, grey plover, jack snipe, **black-tailed godwit,** bar-tailed godwit, green sandpiper, wood sandpiper, spotted redshank, **curlew, common sandpiper, ruff,** black tern.

AVON
---
11 Failand

LOCATION **Four miles (6.5 km) west of Bristol, on the southern side of the A369, overlooking the River Severn.** *Landranger Sheet 172, 518739.*

An attractive, mainly agricultural estate of over 350 acres comprising a patchwork of small fields and sunken lanes, orchards, mature hedgerows and small streams. Patches of varied deciduous woodland add to the mosaic of habitats.

The woodland area has breeding **buzzard,** and sparrowhawk breed nearby.

Despite its proximity to Bristol, the property appears to be little visited and yet represents a rich bird-watching site, well provided with public footpaths.

Highlights
Seventy-six bird species have been recorded, 50 of them breeding species.

Time and season
All year: **heron, mallard, buzzard, kestrel,** pheasant, **lapwing, little owl,** tawny owl, green woodpecker, **skylark, goldcrest, meadow pipit, pied wagtail, goldfinch, linnet, yellowhammer.** Summer: **swallow, swift, sand martin, whinchat, grasshopper warbler, sedge warbler, lesser whitethroat, willow warbler,** chiffchaff, spotted flycatcher and **yellow wagtail.**

THE SOUTH EAST

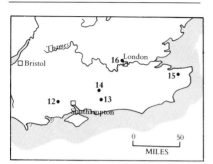

HAMPSHIRE

12 Bramshaw Commons

LOCATION On the northern edge of the New Forest between Bramshaw, Cadnam and Plaitford. Access just south of A36, 10 miles (16 km) west of central Southampton. *Landranger Sheets 184, 185, 270170.*

A series of adjacent commons totalling 1,392 acres. A typical section of New Forest habitat – extensive heath and grassland with bracken, gorse, bogs and areas of mixed woodland.

Highlights
A good range of heathland and woodland birds.

Time and season
All year: **mallard, buzzard, kestrel, red-legged partridge, moorhen, lapwing, woodcock, little owl, pied wagtail, goldcrest, redpoll, yellowhammer.** Winter: **teal, grey wagtail, fieldfare, redwing, rook, reed bunting.** Summer: **redshank, cuckoo,**

nightjar, skylark, meadow pipit, stonechat, Dartford warbler, chiffchaff, **willow warbler.** Passage: **snipe, curlew, black-headed gull, wheatear, goldfinch.**

WEST SUSSEX

13 Petworth Park

LOCATION In Petworth between A272 and A283, five-and-a-half miles (9 km) east of Midhurst. Car park on A283, one-and-a-half miles (2.5 km), north of Petworth. *Landranger Sheet 197, 976218.*

A beautiful 700-acre ancient deer park with a lake, landscaped by 'Capability' Brown. There are also extensive tracts of grassland and woodland. The old trees of the parkland are rich in lichens and hold breeding great spotted and lesser spotted woodpeckers and tawny owl.

Highlights
An interesting location especially for large numbers of birds on passage. The lake is an excellent place to watch feeding **swallows** and martins.

Time and season
All year: **great crested grebe, heron, mallard, tufted duck, Canada goose, mute swan, kestrel, partridge, moorhen, coot, woodcock, rook, goldcrest, pied wagtail, yellowhammer, reed bunting.** Winter: **pochard, snipe, black-headed gull, kingfisher, skylark.** Summer: **swallow,** house martin, **willow**

warbler, spotted flycatcher, **grey wagtail.** Passage: **little grebe, teal, shoveler, goldeneye, buzzard, wheatear, sedge warbler, lesser whitethroat,** chiffchaff and **yellow wagtail.**

SURREY

14 Frensham Common

LOCATION North of Haslemere, astride the A287 2 miles (3 km) north of Churt. After passing Frensham Great Pond there is a car park on the left. *Landranger Sheet 186, 861418.*

An extensive heathland area well scattered with patches of gorse, bracken, birch and pine, two large lakes and smaller pools.

Highlights
Good for scrub warblers and heathland birds; summer evenings for **woodcock, nightjar** and **grasshopper warbler;** winter haunt of great grey shrike.

Time and season
All year: **great crested grebe, little grebe, mallard, tufted duck, partridge, moorhen, coot, lapwing, woodcock, skylark, stonechat, goldcrest, meadow pipit, pied wagtail, goldfinch, redpoll, corn bunting, yellowhammer, linnet.** Winter: **wigeon, teal, shoveler, pintail, goldeneye, black-headed gull, kingfisher,** great grey shrike, **fieldfare, redwing.** Summer: **snipe, nightjar, whinchat, grasshopper**

warbler, sedge warbler, lesser whitethroat, spotted flycatcher, tree pipit, yellow wagtail. Passage: scaup, goosander, buzzard (birds of prey generally), jack snipe, wheatear.

KENT

15 Stodmarsh

LOCATION An area of open water and surrounding reed bed 5 miles (8 km) east of Canterbury. Approach along A257 eastwards towards Sandwich for one mile (1.5 km), then turn left on to unclassified road towards Stodmarsh village. Pass the Red Lion, then turn left along a lane leading to the Reserve car park. Alternative approach via the A28 (Canterbury to Margate road) turning right at Sturry or Upstreet. *Landranger Sheet 179, 221610.*

This National Nature Reserve is the largest freshwater marshland in Kent covering 900 acres, formed by subsidence from nearby coal-mining. An embankment through the Reserve allows a good chance of seeing small, elusive marshland birds. Flooding of the River Stour during winter months extends this wetland to Grove Ferry.

Highlights
Noted for its breeding birds with at least six species of **duck** including **garganey**; also a chance of seeing Cetti's and Savi's warblers.

Time and season
During high summer the path to Grove Ferry tends to be overgrown with nettles and thistles. All year: **bittern, teal, gadwall, garganey, shoveler, pochard, tufted duck, water rail, bearded reedling,** willow tit, **redpoll.** Winter: **wigeon, hen harrier,** ringed plover, **snipe,** water pipit. Summer: **bittern, grasshopper, sedge** and reed **warbler.**

GREATER LONDON

16 Osterley Park

LOCATION West London. Just north of Osterley station (Heathrow branch of the Piccadilly Line). Access from Syon Lane, north side of Great West Road, or from Thornbury Road, just east of the station. *Landranger Sheet 176, 146780.*

Attractive parkland surrounded by farmland. The central Park area also has three, long narrow lakes and there are many interesting shrubs and trees including rare species of oaks. The whole estate represents an oasis for wildlife in a generally suburban setting. There are well-kept bird records for this site which shows it to have an exceptional range of birds both for breeding and for passage.

Highlights
A good chance of seeing, or (at least) hearing breeding **goldcrest,** spotted flycatcher and **corn bunting.** Ring-necked parakeets bred in the park in 1983!

Time and season
The park is most attractive during spring and summer, but interesting bird visitors turn up at all times of the year. All year: **great crested grebe, little grebe, mallard, tufted duck, kestrel, partridge, moorhen, coot, lapwing, goldcrest, pied wagtail, goldfinch, linnet, corn bunting.** Winter: **gadwall, shoveler, kingfisher, fieldfare, redwing, stonechat, meadow pipit, grey wagtail, reed bunting.** Summer: **skylark, swallow,** chiffchaff, spotted flycatcher. Passage: **mute swan, snipe, common sandpiper, sand martin, wheatear, whinchat, lesser whitethroat, willow warbler, yellow wagtail, yellowhammer.**

WALES

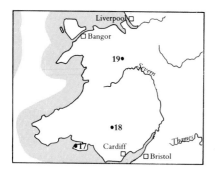

DYFED

17 Ryder's Down

LOCATION On the Gower Peninsula. Take the B4295 to Llanrhidian, then turn in direction of Llangennith, taking first lane on right after Burry. *Landranger Sheet 159, 451920.*

A grazed common with varied bird habitats. The western half is more open with grassland, heath, gorse scrub and a shallow pool. Dense birch and gorse along the northern edge provide useful cover for small birds.

This is one of several National Trust properties on the Gower including sand dune and salt-marsh.

Highlights
A good area for watching scrub birds.

Time and season
All year: **buzzard, skylark, stonechat, meadow pipit, linnet,** yellowhammer. Summer: **cuckoo, willow warbler,** whitethroat.

POWYS

18 Llangorse Lake

LOCATION Eight miles (13 km) east of Brecon. Good general views of the lake from the B4560 Bwlch to Talgarth road. Access to the shore just south of Llangorse and at Llangasty Tal-y-llyn on its southern shore. *Landranger Sheet 161, 135275.*

The largest natural freshwater lake in South Wales.

Highlights
Passage waders and large roosts of **swallows,** martins and **wagtails.**

Time and season
Winter: **little grebe, tufted duck, pochard, Canada goose, whooper swan, Bewick's swan, pied wagtail.** Summer: **great crested grebe, mute swan, swallow,** house martin, **yellow wagtail,** reed warbler, **sedge warbler, reed bunting.** Passage: ringed plover, green sandpiper, wood sandpiper, spotted redshank, sanderling, **ruff.**

CLWYD

19 Erdigg

LOCATION Two miles (3 km) south of Wrexham off the A525. *Landranger Sheet 118, 326482.*

A large agricultural estate which includes a wide scatter of small marl-pit ponds, and areas of rushy grassland and marsh along the valley of the Clywedog River. The varied landscape includes long strips of deciduous woodland.

Highlights
Kingfisher and **dipper** along the river portion, with **grasshopper warbler** associated with tall herb communities around the ponds.

Time and season
Summer for breeding birds. All year: **heron, mallard, buzzard, kestrel, partridge, moorhen, woodcock, barn owl, little owl, kingfisher, dipper, goldcrest, pied wagtail, grey wagtail, goldfinch, linnet, yellowhammer.** Winter: **teal, coot, snipe, fieldfare, redwing.** Summer: **cuckoo, swallow, redstart, whinchat, grasshopper warbler, lesser whitethroat, willow warbler,** chiffchaff, spotted flycatcher.

MIDDLE ENGLAND

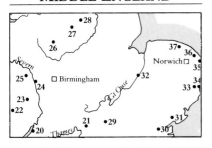

GLOUCESTERSHIRE

20 The New Grounds, Slimbridge

LOCATION On the south-east bank of the River Severn at the head of the estuary; 12 miles (19 km) south of Gloucester, clearly signposted off the A38 (Gloucester to Bristol) road. Bear right after Slimbridge village. Car park on right before entrance to Reserve. *Landranger Sheet 162, 723048.*

Headquarters of the Wildfowl Trust. The reserve covers some 2,000 acres of pools, mud-flats, salt-marsh and low-lying grass fields. Apart from it having the world's largest collection of wildfowl, the refuge is famous for winter **ducks, geese** and **swans**. There are excellent views over the flats from observation towers and hides. Excellent information centre and bookshop. Entrance fee for non-Trust members.

Highlights

Largest wintering flock of **white-fronted geese** in Britain, several hundred **Bewick's swans.**

Time and season

Winter for wildfowl, spring and autumn for passage waders. All year: shelduck, oystercatcher, **curlew,** bar-tailed godwit. Winter: **white-fronted geese, Bewick's swan, teal, wigeon, pintail, shoveler, pochard,** peregrine falcon, grey plover, golden plover, turnstone. Passage: whimbrel, **greenshank, ruff.**

BUCKINGHAMSHIRE

21 Boarstall Duck Decoy

LOCATION On B4011 Thame to Bicester road, 2 miles (3 km) north of Oakley on the western side of the village of Boarstall. *Landranger Sheets 164 or 165, 624151.*

An old duck decoy built in 1697, and used for supplying wild **ducks** to the city of Oxford until as recently as 1950. The decoy pool is surrounded by mixed woodland and scrub including hazel coppice and blackthorn thickets. In the south-western corner of the property is a small pond fringed by willows. Woodland birds include all three species of woodpecker, marsh tit and blackcap. Nature Trail and information centre.

Highlights

Wintering wildfowl.

Time and season

Winter for **ducks,** spring for woodland bird-song and a carpet of woodland flowers. Interesting passage visitors include a white-tailed sea eagle that stayed for several weeks in the vicinity in the winter of 1984/5. All year: **mallard, moorhen.** Winter: **teal, pintail, tufted duck, white-fronted goose, Canada goose, mute swan, kestrel, lapwing, snipe, woodcock, common sandpiper, black-headed gull, kingfisher, fieldfare, redwing.** Summer: **willow warbler,** chiffchaff, spotted flycatcher.

22 Breinton Springs

LOCATION Two miles (3 km) west of Hereford on the northern bank of the River Wye; access via Lower Breinton. *Landranger Sheet 161, 473395.*

Though only 14 acres in extent, the estate includes an old orchard, pond, interesting riverbank vegetation and woodland. The short section of riverbank on the River Wye is an example of a habitat developed as a result of regular flash floods and forms part of the River Wye Site of Special Scientific Interest (SSSI).

The greater part of the property occupies the site of a medieval village.

Highlights

A pleasant spot on the River Wye, the old orchard appeared to be rich in birdlife when the National Trust surveyed the area in May with green woodpecker, robin, **goldcrest,** and **willow warbler.** Also, good for birds of river and riverside eg **sand martins** feeding over river.

Time and season

Summer for a good range of breeding

birds. All year: **mallard, partridge, moorhen, goldcrest, pied wagtail, goldfinch.** Winter: **fieldfare, redwing.** Summer: **cuckoo, sand martin, lesser whitethroat, willow warbler,** chiffchaff, spotted flycatcher.

HEREFORD & WORCESTER

23 Brockhampton

LOCATION Two miles (3 km) east of Bromyard on the A44 Worcester road, then left on a narrow tarmac road through 1½ miles (2.5 km) of woods to Lower Brockhampton, a late-14th-C moated manor house which has its own small car park. Verge parking also allowed on the west of the property on the common alongside Warren Wood. *Landranger Sheet 149, 682546.*

Over 1,500 acres of undulating Herefordshire countryside with farmland, grassland and steep-sided wooded valleys. The outlying area to the north of Tedstone Delamere has herb-rich grassland, orchards, and a small pocket of wetland.

The native woodland supports a large number of breeding birds including sparrowhawk, **buzzard,** raven and pied flycatcher. A nature walk through the woodland of Holly Bank has an accompanying information leaflet available from the local National Trust office.

Highlights
An attractive area for sightings of farmland and woodland birds.

Time and season
All year: **little grebe, mallard, partridge, moorhen, coot, kestrel, red-legged partridge, lapwing, woodcock, little owl,** green woodpecker, **meadow pipit, skylark, pied wagtail, goldfinch, linnet, yellowhammer.** Summer: **cuckoo, willow warbler,** chiffchaff, spotted flycatcher.

---

24 Kinver Edge

LOCATION Four miles (6.5 km) west of Stourbridge and 4 miles (6.5 km) north of Kidderminster; access west of A449. *Landranger Sheet 138, 835830.*

This beautiful estate lies on the western edge of the Birmingham Plateau, an area mainly of red sandstone. A varied property of heath dotted with scrub and birch and mixed woodland. Old hawthorn bushes draped with lichens provide particularly useful nest sites.

The woodland holds breeding great spotted, lesser spotted and green woodpeckers, also wood warbler.

Highlights
Excellent variety of heath and birch scrub birds within 10 miles (16 km) of the centre of Birmingham.

Time and season
Spring and summer for nesting birds; in autumn blue, long-tailed coal, and marsh tits feed in mixed parties at the woodland edge. All year: **kestrel, woodcock, barn owl, little owl,** long-eared owl, rook, goldcrest, yellowhammer. Winter: **fieldfare, redwing.** Summer: **cuckoo, willow warbler,** chiffchaff.

SHROPSHIRE

25 Dudmaston

LOCATION Four miles (6.5 km) south-east of Bridgnorth on the A442 Kidderminster road. *Landranger Sheet 138, 746887.*

An extensive estate of over 3,000 acres includes six farms, a landscaped park with woodland and, most interesting for birdlife, a series of four pools with fringing vegetation. The estate also includes a one-and-a-half mile (2.5 km) stretch of the left bank of the River Severn.

The woodland holds six species of tits, great and lesser spotted woodpecker, nuthatch and treecreeper.

Dudmaston Hall has fine contents.

Highlights
Water birds and passage migrants.

Time and season
All year: **great crested grebe, little grebe, mallard, teal, tufted duck, pochard, Canada goose, mute swan, kestrel, partridge, moorhen, coot, snipe, barn owl, little owl, kingfisher, goldcrest, pied wagtail, yellowhammer, reed bunting.** Winter: cormorant, **wigeon, shoveler and goldeneye.** Summer: **cuckoo,** chiffchaff, spotted flycatcher, **yellow wagtail.** Passage: osprey, **redshank,**

common sandpiper, sand martin, lesser whitethroat.

26 Dovedale

LOCATION Four miles (6.5 km) north of Ashbourne; take A515 for 1 mile (1.5 km), then left via Thorpe; car park facilities. *Landranger Sheet 119, 140530.*

A deep valley that cuts into a limestone plateau – a famous beauty spot. The 1,300 acre property includes limestone outcrops, crags, pinnacles and spires, areas of grassland, the banks of the River Dove itself and some lovely stretches of ancient ash woodland, particularly on the west side of the valley. Woodland birds include green and great spotted woodpecker, **redstart**, spotted flycatcher, (pied flycatcher has nested in the past).

Dovedale is famous not only as a beauty spot, but for its association with Isaak Walton, author of *The Compleat Angler.*

Highlights
Wagtails and **dipper** where the water flows fast.

Time and season
Spring and early summer for bird song and activity in a picturesque valley setting. All year: **mallard, kestrel, partridge, moorhen, rook, dipper, goldcrest, grey wagtail, yellow-hammer.** Winter: **heron, kingfisher, fieldfare, redwing.** Summer: **common sandpiper, redstart, willow warbler,** spotted flycatcher, **linnet, pied wagtail.**

DERBYSHIRE

27 Hardwick Hall

LOCATION Six-and-a-half miles (10.5 km) north-west of Mansfield, 9½ miles (15.5 km) south-east of Chesterfield; approach from M1 (junction 29) on A617. *Landranger Sheet 120, 463638.*

A large and varied estate of over 2,000 acres, made up of park and farmland. Most interesting are Miller's and Great Ponds on the western part of the estate and Car Ponds, along the estate's north-eastern edge which were formed by the damming of the River Doe Lea. These pockets of wetland generally have a good aquatic vegetation including alder carr and willow scrub. Woodland on the estate includes breeding blackcap, garden warbler and bullfinch. A Nature Trail leaflet is available from the local office of the National Trust and from the Information Centre situated on the extreme western part of the estate between Great Pond and Miller's Pond.

Highlights
A good range of wetland, parkland and grassland birds.

Time and season
All year: **great crested grebe, little grebe, mallard, Canada goose, kestrel, red-legged partridge, partridge, moorhen, coot, woodcock, little owl, skylark, goldcrest, meadow pipit, pied wagtail, grey wagtail, goldfinch, reed bunting.** Winter: **heron, pochard, mute swan,** lapwing, snipe, kingfisher, fieldfare, redwing, siskin, **linnet, redpoll, yellowhammer.** Summer: **cuckoo, swallow, willow warbler,** chiffchaff, spotted flycatcher. Passage: golden plover, **tree pipit, yellow wagtail.**

NOTTINGHAMSHIRE

28 Clumber Park

LOCATION Two-and-a-half miles (4 km) south-east of Worksop, 4½ miles (7 km) south-west of Retford, between A614 and B6005. **Several entrances: A57 Manton Lodge; A614 Apley Head Lodge, Normanton Gate and Drayton Gate; B6005 Carbunton crossroads; B6005 Clumber Lane End.** *Landranger Sheet 120, 645774 or 626746.*

One of the several great Midland estates known collectively as the Dukeries, Clumber Park covers over 3,700 acres of parkland, meadow, heath and woodland. The estate was laid out in the late-18th C by 'Capability' Brown from the heathland edge of Sherwood Forest. Clumber Lake and the River Poulter add to the diversity of habitats and make this an exceptionally rich bird-watching site.

Regular breeding birds of the extensive woodland areas include sparrow-hawk, **long-eared owl** and the elusive hawfinch.

Highlights
Winter wildfowl, passage migrants and a good list of breeding birds.

Time and season
All year: **heron, Canada goose, mallard, teal, shoveler, tufted duck, pochard, moorhen, coot, lapwing, snipe, woodcock, kingfisher, rook, skylark, whinchat, meadow pipit, tree pipit, pied wagtail, yellow wagtail, redpoll, yellowhammer, reed bunting.** Winter: great northern diver, cormorant, **bittern, wigeon, pintail, goldeneye, red-breasted merganser,** goosander, pink-footed goose, **white-fronted goose, mute swan, whooper swan, Bewick's swan, water rail, fieldfare, redwing.** Summer: **common sandpiper, cuckoo, nightjar, redstart, nightingale, grasshopper warbler,** reed warbler, **sedge warbler, lesser whitethroat, willow warbler,** chiffchaff, spotted flycatcher, **whinchat, tree pipit, yellow wagtail.** Passage: Slavonian grebe, black-necked grebe, **garganey,** common scoter, **curlew,** bar-tailed godwit, **greenshank,** dunlin.

HERTFORDSHIRE

29 Ashridge

LOCATION **Three miles (5 km) north of Berkhamsted between A41 and B489, astride B4506.** *Landranger Sheet 165, 980120.*

Lying only 28 miles (45 km) north of London, Ashridge Park covers nearly 4,000 acres, encompassing parts of Buckinghamshire, Bedfordshire and Hertfordshire. Its main features are chalk downland with beech hangers, scrub-heath with silver birch, hawthorn, gorse, heather and bracken, and ancient woodland – mainly oak, beech and hornbeam.

Breeding woodland birds include sparrowhawk, great and lesser spotted woodpeckers and hawfinch, the latter bird associated with stands of hornbeam and wild cherry. Other interesting woodland wildlife includes both common and edible dormouse.

Highlights
Interesting range of grass, scrub and woodland birds.

Time and season
Tends to get crowded on spring and summer weekends, best to reach the site early in the day. All year: **mallard, red-legged partridge, partridge, lapwing, woodcock, little owl, skylark, rook, goldcrest, meadow pipit, pied wagtail, goldfinch, linnet, redpoll, corn bunting, yellowhammer, reed bunting.** Winter: **teal, black-headed gull, fieldfare, redwing.** Summer: **whinchat, redstart, grasshopper warbler, sedge warbler, lesser whitethroat, tree pipit.**

ESSEX

30 Danbury and Lingwood Commons

LOCATION **Five miles (8 km) east of Chelmsford. Danbury Common lies just south of Danbury village alongside the A414. The smaller area of Lingwood Common lies just to the north of Danbury.** *Landranger Sheet 167, 780050.*

Two interesting areas of grassland, heath, scrub, and oak-birch woodland. Scrub-woodland is particularly well developed at the centre of Lingwood Common, with dense tangles of brambles, briars and climbers. Hawthorn and blackthorn thickets add to the diversity of nesting sites. **Red-backed shrike** has been reported in the past as a breeding species, but is no longer present. The wooded areas have all three species of woodpecker, hawfinch and **nightingale.**

Both commons have open access with a large number of footpaths and bridleways.

Highlights
A good place to see heath, scrub and woodland birds. This mixed habitat is becoming rare in Essex.

Time and season
Summer for breeding birds. All year: **red-legged partridge, moorhen, woodcock, little owl, goldcrest, pied wagtail, linnet, redpoll, yellowhammer.** Winter: **short-eared owl, fieldfare, redwing.** Summer: **lesser whitethroat, willow warbler,** chiffchaff, spotted flycatcher.

---

31 Abberton Reservoir

LOCATION **Four miles (6.5 km) south of Colchester on the B1026 (Colchester to Maldon) which leads across the middle section of the Reservoir; a minor road leading back to the village of Layer Breton also crosses the water.** *Landranger Sheet 168, 970180.*

One of the finest reservoirs for bird-watching in the country. It covers 1,240 acres and is divided into three sections; the largest is embanked by concrete but holds extremely large numbers of **ducks**. The upper two sections with natural banks also attract a variety of waders. A causeway crossing the main section of the reservoir has an enclosure containing a small collection of European wildfowl. There is also a public hide which overlooks a wide bay with artificial islands attracting both breeding ducks and terns. Access to the reservoir banks is limited to members of the Essex Bird Watching and Preservation Society.

Highlights
Outstanding for the number and variety of autumn and winter wildfowl, especially **ducks**; the numbers of **mallard, shoveler, tufted duck, pochard** and **goldeneye** are among the highest in Britain.

Time and season
Winter: **mallard, gadwall, wigeon, pintail, shoveler**, red-crested pochard, scaup, **tufted duck, pochard, goldeneye**, goosander, smew, **white-fronted goose, Bewick's swan**. Autumn: **garganey, greenshank, ruff**, common, Arctic and black terns.

CAMBRIDGESHIRE

32 Ouse Washes

LOCATION In the Fens between the parallel channels of the Old and New Bedford Rivers. From Chat-teris take the B1908 to Horseway; on the 90° bend just after the village, having crossed the Forty Foot Drain, turn right on to the minor road and continue to Welches Dam (signposted from Manea). Car park and visitors' centre. *Landranger Sheet 156, 478677.*

An interesting area at all times for their strange, haunting beauty, the Ouse Washes cover a 20-mile (32-km) long series of meadows on the western side of the River Ouse. They represent the largest area of regularly flooded grazing marshland in Britain and are an internationally important site for over-wintering wildfowl. Apart from the meadows, the area includes the river and ditches, osier beds and willow holts. The Wildfowl Trust, RSPB and the Cambridge and Isle of Ely Naturalists' Trust (Cambient) all own section of the Washes.

Highlights
The stirring sight of up to 2,500 **Bewick's swans** in winter; this is also the main British breeding site for **black-tailed godwit**.

Time and season
The meadows flood regularly each winter attracting a wealth of wildfowl; spring for jousting **ruff** and summer for breeding marshland birds. All year: **little grebe**, heron, **mallard, teal, gadwall, pintail, shoveler, tufted duck, pochard**, goosander, **red-breasted merganser, snipe, black-tailed godwit**, little owl, short-eared owl. Winter: **great crested grebe, Bewick's swan, wigeon** (over 40,000), **whooper swan, white-fronted goose, water rail, kingfisher, fieldfare, redwing**. Summer: **garganey**, shelduck, **lapwing, redshank, ruff, yellow wagtail** (several hundred pairs), **reed warbler, goldfinch** and **redpoll**.

SUFFOLK

33 Dunwich Heath

LOCATION Turn south off the Westleton to Dunwich road half-a-mile (0.8 km) before reaching Dunwich. *Landranger Sheet 156, 475683.*

An area of coastal heath covering some 214 acres and lying just to the north of the RSPB's famous Minsmere Reserve. This attractive heathland property consists largely of bracken and heather, interspersed with clumps of gorse, and scrub made up of predominantly silver birch saplings. Many tracks criss-cross the Reserve and there is access to the beach.

Highlights
Nightjar song and courtship flights on summer evenings; **stone curlew**.

Time and season
Summer for breeding heathland birds, autumn and winter for migrant warblers and wildfowl. All year: **kestrel, partridge, red-legged partridge, skylark, stonechat, meadow pipit, pied wagtail, linnet, goldfinch, redpoll, yellowhammer**. Summer: **stone curlew, cuckoo, nightjar,**

swallow, sand martin, lesser whitethroat, willow warbler, wheatear, whinchat, tree pipit, yellow wagtail.

34 Minsmere

LOCATION In Westleton, 5 miles (8 km) north-east of Saxmundham; follow signs to Dunwich. After one-and-three-quarter miles (2.5 km) turn right at signs for Dunwich Heath and Minsmere; car park where tarmac road ends. *Landranger Sheet 156, 478677.*

Probably the best all-round bird-watching site in southern England. The 1,500 acre Reserve includes reed-swamp, meadow, an area of lagoons known as 'The Scrape', heathland scrub and woodland. The woodland birds, including the three native species of woodpecker, are best seen in the spring before the tree canopy becomes too dense. Over 300 species have been recorded, with 100 breeding species. The reserve is adjacent to the National Trust property, Dunwich Heath.

Highlights
A classic site for breeding **avocet**.

Time and season
Something of interest throughout the year, but late summer and autumn for a great variety of water birds including ocasional rare visitors such as spoonbill and purple heron. All year: **heron, bittern, marsh harrier, water rail, avocet, kingfisher, bearded reedling**. Winter: **red-throated diver,**

scoter, eider, **hen harrier.** Summer: **garganey, gadwall, shoveler, redstart, nightingale, red-backed shrike,** Cetti's warbler, reed warbler, **sedge warbler, grasshopper warbler, corn bunting.** Passage: spotted redshank, little stint, **black-tailed godwit,** bar-tailed godwit and **ruff.**

35 Breydon Water

LOCATION **Immediately behind Great Yarmouth. There is a public footpath on the southern side of the Water, linking Great Yarmouth with Burgh Castle. The path starts from the northern end of town; take the first turning right across Southtown Bridge. Access to the northern side of Breydon Water is by a lane that leads from Freethorpe village on the B1140 (Acle to Reedham road) to the Berney Arms Inn, from where a public footpath runs along the north bank.** *Landranger Sheet 134, 522075.*

A tidal estuary with only a narrow access to the sea, Breydon Water cover some 1,900 acres with extensive mud-flats, salt-marsh and pasture land.

Highlights
This location is known for the great variety of waders and wildfowl on migration; a small flock of bean geese, whose main wintering area is on the River Yare, often visit.

Time and season
Winter: **wigeon,** shelduck, **pintail,**

shoveler, scaup, **goldeneye,** bean goose, Brent goose, **white-fronted goose,** pink-footed goose, **Bewick's swan, marsh harrier, hen harrier, short-eared owl,** snow bunting, Lapland bunting. Passage: **curlew,** whimbrel, bar-tailed godwit, **black-tailed godwit,** green sandpiper, wood sandpiper, **ruff.**

NORFOLK

36 Horsey Mere

LOCATION **Eleven miles (17.5 km) north of Yarmouth astride the B1159. The focus of bird-watching activity is Horsey Mere, viewed by stopping at the windmill half-a-mile (0.8 km) south of Horsey village, from where a public footpath leads round the north-eastern side of the Mere. Access to other parts by application only to regional National Trust office.** *Landranger Sheet 134, 460230.*

The Mere with its extensive reed-beds and fen, together with nearby Hickling Broad (a National Nature Reserve), comprise the largest area of reed-swamp on the Norfolk Broads. This is one of East Anglia's prime bird sites. Nearness to the coast adds interest, with a great influx of terns and waders on spring and autumn migration.

Highlights
Apart from its wealth of marshland birds, proximity to the sea results in many small migrants sheltering in the shrubs behind the dunes. Rare sightings

include Slavonian grebe and spoonbill.

Time and season

Notable for winter wildfowl and raptors, breeding marsh-birds and passage migrants in spring and autumn. All year: **great crested grebe, heron, bittern, mute swan, teal, mallard, partridge, water rail, moorhen, coot, lapwing, redshank, snipe, kingfisher, bearded reedling, reed bunting, pied wagtail,** marsh tit. Winter: **Bewick's swan, whooper swan,** smew, **hen harrier,** peregrine falcon, bar-tailed godwit, **greenshank,** jack snipe, **ruff,** ringed plover. Summer: **garganey, shoveler, marsh harrier,** corncrake, **yellow wagtail, grasshopper warbler,** reed warbler, **sedge warbler, willow warbler.** Passage: **marsh harrier,** black tern, **black-tailed godwit, common** and wood **sandpipers, greenshank, ruff.**

37 Blickling

LOCATION One-and-a-half miles (2.5 km) north-west of Aylsham on the north side of the B1354. There is a car park near the Hall open from April to October. Additional car parks lie just off the Ingworth to Itteringham road at Park Farm. *Landranger Sheet 133, 170280.*

A large estate with a considerable lake, fringed with reed-beds. The farmland has an attractive mix of wet meadowland, drains and alder woodland. There is also some heath. An information leaflet gives details of a circular walk through the estate.

Highlights

A varied range of both farmland and wetland birds. Wildfowl on the lake in winter and on close-turfed area on its eastern side.

Time and season

All year: **great crested grebe, little grebe, mallard,** shelduck, Egyptian goose, **Canada goose, kestrel, red-legged partridge, partridge, moorhen, coot, lapwing, snipe, woodcock, little owl, kingfisher,** green woodpecker, **skylark, goldcrest, pied wagtail, goldfinch, linnet, redpoll, reed bunting.** Winter: Cormorant, **teal, tufted duck, pochard, goldeneye, red-breasted merganser, goosander, greylag goose,** Brent goose, **marsh harrier, hen harrier, woodlark, fieldfare, redwing, grey wagtail,** siskin, **corn bunting.** Summer: **common sandpiper, cuckoo, swift,** reed warbler, **willow warbler,** chiffchaff, spotted flycatcher, **tree pipit.**

NORTHERN ENGLAND

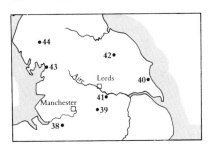

GREATER MANCHESTER

38 Tatton Park

LOCATION Twelve miles (19 km) south-west of Manchester and 3½ miles, (5.5 km) north of Knutsford; entrance on A5034 just north of junction of A5034 and A50. *Landranger Sheets 109 and 118, 737815.*

The focus of the Park is two adjacent meres, Melchett Mere and the much more extensive, mile-long (1.5 km) Tatton Mere. Both stretches of water have a lush growth of aquatic plants, with a large area of fen and reed-swamp at the southern end of Tatton Mere (Knutsford Moor) that holds breeding sedge and reed warblers. There is also an area of mixed woodland at the south-eastern corner of the estate.

These meres, two of many in the area, were formed some 15,000 years ago by movements of the ice sheet that covered the Cheshire-Shropshire plain. Rostherne Mere, a National Nature Reserve, and probably the best freshwater-bird site in the county, lies just 2 miles (3.2 km) to the north between Knutsford and Altrincham.

Regular winter sea-bird visitors to Tatton Mere include: great northern diver, cormorant, great black-backed gull, Arctic tern and black tern.

Highlights
Winter wildfowl.

Time and season
All year: **great crested grebe, little grebe, mallard, teal, tufted duck, Canada goose, mute swan, kestrel, moorhen, coot, lapwing, redshank, little owl, skylark, goldcrest, meadow pipit, pied wagtail, grey wagtail, yellow wagtail, redpoll, yellowhammer, reed bunting.** Winter: black-necked grebe, **heron, gadwall, wigeon, shoveler,** scaup, **pochard, goldeneye,** eider, goosander, shelduck, pink-footed goose, **Bewick's swan,** peregrine falcon, **snipe, woodcock, curlew, common sandpiper, ruff, fieldfare, redwing.** Summer: **cuckoo, swallow, sand martin, grasshopper warbler, sedge warbler,** reed warbler, **willow warbler,** chiffchaff, spotted flycatcher.

SOUTH YORKSHIRE

39 Worsbrough Mill Country Park

LOCATION **Two miles (3 km) south of Barnsley on the A61, car park adjacent to the main road.** *Landranger Sheet 110, 350033.*

This small yet interesting area features the open water and reed-beds of Worsbrough Reservoir with its surrounding woodland and farmland. A hide on the north-west bank of the Reservoir gives interesting views of a muddy spit where migrating waders tend to congregate. Woodland birds include lesser spotted woodpecker, willow tit and blackcap.

Highlights
Passage migrants and good range of breeding water birds.

Time and season
Spring and autumn for passage migrants, including large **swallow** roost; good range of breeding birds. Winter: **pochard, goldeneye** (uncommon). Summer: **heron, great crested grebe, little grebe, mallard, tufted duck, partridge, coot, moorhen, water rail,** reed warbler, **willow warbler,** spotted flycatcher, **goldfinch.** Passage: **lapwing,** little ringed plover, **snipe, common sandpiper, greenshank.**

HUMBERSIDE

40 Hornsea Mere

LOCATION **Twelve miles (19 km) south of Bridlington beside the B1242 just outside the village of Hornsea.** *Landranger Sheet 107, 188471.*

The feature of this RSPB reserve is the Mere itself, a 2-mile (3 km) long nutrient-rich lake with extensive reed-swamp at its western end. Close proximity to the sea adds to the attraction of this prime bird-watching site. Of the many sea-bird visitors, the large winter roost of cormorants is of note; also the presence of little gulls in late summer.

Highlights
A great variety of wildfowl including a spring gathering of **goldeneye** and late summer moult of **mute swans.**

Time and season
All year: **mute swan, mallard, pochard, tufted duck, shoveler, gadwall.** Winter: **wigeon, goldeneye, water rail, coot** (often in very large numbers), **bearded reedling.** Summer: reed warbler, **sedge warbler,** reed bunting. Passage: **ruff, greenshank, wheatear, whinchat.**

WEST YORKSHIRE

41 Fairburn Ings

LOCATION **Two miles (3 km) north of Ferrybridge, west of Fairburn on the A1.** *Landranger Sheet 105, 450275.*

An RSPB wetland reserve in a largely industrial landscape, the main bodies of water having been formed by mining subsidence. The western end of the Reserve is mainly agricultural land with several shallow pools. This end of the Reserve tends to flood in winter attracting wildfowl. The whole Reserve is interesting for the variety of habitats including an old canal, a reclaimed slag bank (**willow warblers** breeding in the birches), small patches of reed-beds, and slag heaps and slurry ponds.

Highlights

Whooper swans and large **gull** roost in winter, passage and breeding waders.

Time and season

All year: **gadwall, shoveler, pochard, lapwing, snipe, redshank, black-headed gull.** Winter: **whooper swan, goldeneye,** goosander, **fieldfare, redwing.** Summer: **garganey,** reed warbler, **willow warbler, lesser whitethroat.** Passage: **water rail, common sandpiper, greenshank,** swallow, sand martin.

NORTH YORKSHIRE

42 Bransdale

LOCATION Six miles (10 km) north of Helmsley, approach via A170. *Landranger Sheet 100, 620980.*

An isolated U-shaped valley set in the North Yorkshire Moors, Bransdale covers over 1,900 acres of mainly agricultural land with small scattered farmsteads and gently curving field walls. Bird habitats include extensive areas of rough and wet grassland, streamsides and patches of oak woodland. The proximity of the moor allows for regular sightings of birds such as merlin and golden plover. The area is altogether delightful, a secluded valley with a fine range of breeding birds.

Highlights

Three species of **wagtail** as breeding birds, snow buntings are regular winter visitors and rough-legged buzzard frequently seen on passage, spring/autumn.

Time and season

The drumming of **snipe** and call of **curlew** are evocative in spring and early summer. All year: **heron, mallard, teal, kestrel, red-legged partridge, partridge, moorhen, coot, dipper, meadow pipit, pied wagtail, grey wagtail, goldfinch, linnet, yellowhammer.** Winter: **fieldfare, redwing.** Summer: **lapwing, snipe, curlew, common sandpiper, cuckoo, short-eared owl, kingfisher, swallow, sand martin, yellowhammer, wheatear, whinchat, grasshopper warbler, sedge warbler, willow warbler,** chiffchaff, **goldcrest, tree pipit, pied wagtail, grey wagtail, yellow wagtail, redpoll.** Passage: **hen harrier.**

Lake District

Over a quarter of the Lake District National Park is owned by the National Trust including six of the main lakes with much of their shoreline. Away from the more popular tourist areas, the lakes are interesting for a variety of waterfowl. Patches of wet woodland, reed-bed and the banks of numerous streams add to the variety of wetland bird-watching sites.

Breeding species

The Lake District is the best English location for both goosander and **red-breasted merganser,** which expanded their breeding ranges southwards from Scotland in the 1950s and 1960s. Both species are quite common on the Trust's larger lakes. Goosander tend to nest in old trees by the water's edge, also among boulders. **Goldeneye,** another tree-nesting species turn up sporadically during the summer, but as yet breeding has not been confirmed.

Great crested grebe (scarce in Northern England) breeds regularly at Blelham Tarn (north-east of Hawkshead), Moss Eccles Tarn (west of Windermere) and on Loweswater.

Bearded reedling has been recorded at Elterwater (south of Ambleside).

Three of the most common birds associated with running water are **common sandpiper, dipper** and **grey wagtail,** and the Lake District has many streams and riversides where these species can be seen.

Wintering species

Commonest winter visitors include **great crested grebe, little grebe, mallard, teal, tufted duck, pochard, goldeneye** and **coot.** Small parties of **whooper swans** regularly show up but stay on the lakes for only short periods. Less frequent visitors include black-throated diver, black-necked grebe and Slavonian grebe, scaup and smew.

The most interesting lakes for wildfowl are Windermere (large numbers of **tufted duck, goldeneye** and **coot**), Derwentwater (shelduck at southern end during moult migration) and Brothers Water (for a great variety of wildfowl on a relatively small area).

Cormorant are present on many lakes and tarns outside the breeding season; the largest roost is at Ladyholm on Windermere.

LANCASHIRE

43 Leighton Moss

LOCATION Four miles (6.5 km) north of Carnforth near the village of Silverdale. Access from exit 35 of M6 then A6 heading north. After 3 miles (5 km) turn left on to a minor road via Yealand Redmayne. *Landranger Sheet 97, 478751.*

An attractive, mainly wetland reserve that occupies the floor of a small, unspoilt wooded valley, once an arm of Morecambe Bay. Managed by the RSPB, it covers over 300 acres of open water, reed-swamp, fen edge, willow scrub and oak and ash woodland. A bridleway runs along the causeway between Leighton Moss and Storrs Moss. There are several hides and an information centre.

Highlights
The only northern location with regular breeding populations of both **bittern** and reed warbler.

Time and season
The **bittern's** booming call can be heard from the middle of January until midsummer. The best time to see the birds themselves is early summer when the parents are actively foraging. All year: **teal, gadwall, shoveler, pochard, tufted duck,** sparrowhawk, **kestrel, water rail, woodcock, barn owl, bearded reedling, reed bunting.** Winter: **wigeon, pintail, goldeneye, redpoll.** Summer: **garganey, black-headed gull, grasshopper warbler,** reed warbler, **sedge warbler, lesser whitethroat.** Autumn: spotted redshank, **greenshank, ruff, swallow** and **sand martin** (in large numbers), **pied wagtail, yellow wagtail.**

CUMBRIA

44 Hartsop and Caudale

LOCATION Two-and-a-half miles (4 km) south of Patterdale, west of A592. *Landranger Sheet 90, 400100.*

A property of nearly 3,500 acres at the head of Patterdale, one of the most picturesque valleys in the Lake District. The estate includes two tarns – Brothers Water and a section of the shore of Hawswater – scattered meadowland, small rocky streams, woodland, grass-heath slopes, and upland crags and screes. Brothers Water with its reed-beds and surrounding woodland is a particularly rich bird site. Upland birds are well represented and include breeding **buzzard,** red grouse, raven and ring ouzel. Woodland birds include coal tit, tree creeper and pied flycatcher.

Highlights
The lake supports an excellent variety of water-birds, breeding and wintering.

Time and season
Wide variety of birds can be seen on passage. All year: **heron, mallard, teal, red-breasted merganser, buzzard, kestrel, partridge, moorhen, coot, snipe, woodcock, curlew, barn owl, dipper, goldfinch, linnet, redpoll, yellowhammer.** Winter and passage: **little grebe, wigeon, pintail, tufted duck, pochard, goldeneye, goosander, shelduck, mute swan, whooper swan, Bewick's swan, water rail,** jack snipe, green sandpiper, **greenshank, dunlin, black-headed gull, short-eared owl, sand martin,** rook, fieldfare, redwing. Summer: **common sandpiper, redshank, kingfisher, skylark, swallow, wheatear, whinchat, redstart, sedge warbler, willow warbler,** chiffchaff, goldcrest, spotted flycatcher, **meadow pipit, tree pipit, pied wagtail, grey wagtail, yellow wagtail.**

SCOTLAND

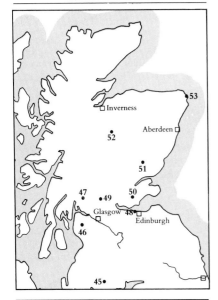

DUMFRIES & GALLOWAY

45 Threave

LOCATION Two miles (3 km) south-west of Castle Douglas on A75. *Landranger Sheet 83, 760620.*

Threave Wildfowl Refuge occupies the low ground of the River Dee, part of the attractive Threave Estate, famous for its gardens. The Refuge, which is open from November to March, has four hides, two beside the river, a third on an island in the river, and a fourth between the river and Carlingwark Loch. An information leaflet is available from the Warden.

Nearby Loch Ken is also worth investigating for winter wildfowl.

Highlights

Greylag geese on rough grazed farmland, diving ducks on the river.

Time and season

Winter: **heron, little grebe, greylag goose, gadwall, wigeon, pintail, shoveler,** scaup, **goldeneye, gadwall,** smew, **white-fronted goose,** bean goose, pink-footed goose, **whooper swan.**

STRATHCLYDE

46 Lochwinnoch

LOCATION Fifteen miles (24 km) south-west of Glasgow; take A737 to Barr Castle then A760 for just over one mile (1.5 km) to Lochwinnoch. *Landranger Sheet 63, 355583.*

The shallow water and marshy fringes of Barr Loch and Aird Meadow form the centre of this RSPB Reserve covering 388 acres. In summer, the lochs support a rich growth of water plants, and the surrounding marshes abound with **sedge warblers.** There are islands with nesting **duck** and **gulls.** Three small areas of woodland hold breeding sparrowhawk and the great spotted woodpecker.

This well-managed Reserve has a fine information centre, observation tower, nature trail and two hides.

Highlights

Wildfowl in winter, but also all year round as an interesting bird site with back-up information, within easy access of Glasgow.

Time and season

All year: **mallard, tufted duck, pochard, shoveler, coot.** Winter: **teal, wigeon, goldeneye,** smew, **greylag goose, whooper swan,** Bewick's swan. Summer: **great crested grebe, water rail, black-headed gull, rook, grasshopper warbler, sedge warbler, yellow wagtail, reed bunting.**

47 Loch Lomond

LOCATION Eighteen miles (29 km) north-west of Glasgow. Take A809, then B837 at Drymen to Balmaha. *Landranger Sheet 56, 420080.*

A famous beauty spot, Loch Lomond stretches for over 20 miles (32 km). The south-eastern corner of the Loch is especially interesting for birds and much of this area forms part of a National Nature Reserve. In particular, the marshes and pools bordering Endrick Water are attractive for winter wildfowl including **wigeon** and **whooper swan.** There is a **heronry** at Balmaha. Also of interest for their marsh and woodland birds are the Montrose Estates (Buchanan Castle); permission to visit this site needs to be obtained from the Factor's Office in Drymen.

Highlights

A picturesque area with a rich variety of waterfowl, waders and woodland birds.

Time and season

Early summer for breeding warblers, autumn and winter for wildfowl and waders on the Loch and surrounding marshes. Winter: **wigeon, shoveler,** pochard, tufted duck, red-breasted merganser, goldeneye, smew (on Endrick Water and adjacent pools), greylag goose, white-fronted goose, whooper swan. Summer: mallard, teal, red-breasted merganser, woodcock, common sandpiper, long-eared owl, redstart, grasshopper warbler, chiffchaff, grey wagtail, redpoll. Passage: garganey, marsh harrier, black-tailed godwit, green sandpiper.

LOTHIAN

48 Duddingston Loch

LOCATION Within Holyrood Park, one-and-a-half miles (2.5 km) from the centre of Edinburgh. Landranger Sheet 66, 280730.

A 30-acre Reserve of natural loch and reed-bed with surrounding scrub, meadow and moorland – all within a short walk from the centre of Edinburgh. Public access from Queens Drive which encircles the Park, also excellent views of the Loch from Duddingston foreshore where the Loch meets the Park, close to Duddingston Road. Elsewhere access is restricted; further information from the Ministry of Public Buildings and Works.

Highlights
Over 5,000 pochard roost on the Loch in winter, flying out each evening to feed in the nearby Firth of Forth.

Time and season
All year: great crested grebe,

mallard, teal, tufted duck, pochard. Winter: shoveler, goldeneye, water rail. Summer: little grebe, mute swan, moorhen, coot, long-eared owl, sedge warbler, willow warbler, redpoll, reed bunting.

CENTRAL

49 Flanders Moss

LOCATION Eighteen miles (29 km) west of Stirling on A811; best approach from Buchlyvie at the junction of A811 and B835. Landranger Sheet 57, 550040.

This, the largest raised peat bog in Scotland, includes the upper reaches of the River Forth with the Lake of Menteith at its north-eastern corner. The whole area is one of great open spaces, with unbroken views of Ben Ledi and Ben Vorlich to the north. Black grouse, with capercaillie in the woodland south of the lake.

Highlights
West Flanders Moss has a huge black-headed gullery. The area attracts large numbers of geese in winter and is generally interesting for its wide range of raptors.

Time and season
All year: buzzard, hen harrier, black-headed gull, merlin, short-eared owl. Winter: goldeneye, greylag goose, pink-footed goose, whooper swan, great grey shrike. Summer: heron, goosander, woodcock, curlew.

FIFE

50 Loch Leven

LOCATION Just east of Kinross between the Firth of Forth and the Firth of Tay. The best views of the Loch are from the southern side at Vane Farm (RSPB Reserve), on the B9097 which runs from Junction 5 on the M90 (Edinburgh to Kinross) Motorway to Balingry and Glenrothes. Landranger Sheet 58, 150010.

A huge freshwater-loch of over 3,900 acres including six islands. This National Nature Reserve is an important wildfowl site with the largest numbers of breeding duck (mainly tufted and mallard) in the country. Apart from Vane Farm, main access to the water's edge is from Kirkgate Pass, signposted from the centre of Kinross.

Highlights
Several thousand greylag and pink-footed geese roost on the water and feed on surrounding farmland during the autumn. At the same time large flocks of fieldfare and redwing feed on rowan berries in the woods bordering the lake.

Time and season
Autumn and winter for wildfowl. All year: greylag goose, mallard, tufted duck, wigeon, shoveler. Winter: pochard, goldeneye, goosander, whooper swan, fieldfare, redwing. Summer: gadwall, shelduck, mute swan. Passage: bean goose, greenshank, ruff.

TAYSIDE

51 Loch of Kinnordy

LOCATION Two miles (3 km) west of Kirriemuir. The B951 road heading west passes close to the southern side of the Loch. *Landranger Sheet 54, 360540.*

The Loch covers some 165 acres and though formerly much larger was reduced in size by partial drainage in the last century. The Loch and its hinterland is now an RSPB Reserve with extensive fen, floating bog and a thin strip of woodland along its southern edge.

Highlights
Breeding water-birds including a **black-headed gullery** of some 6,000 pairs. Ruddy duck has nested in the past.

Time and season
All year: **mallard, teal, shoveler, tufted duck, pochard, black-headed gull.** Winter: **wigeon, gadwall, greylag goose.** Summer: **great crested grebe, moorhen, coot, snipe, woodcock, black-headed gull, long-eared owl, sedge warbler, willow warbler, reed bunting.** Passage: **lapwing, curlew, common sandpiper, redshank, ruff.**

HIGHLAND

52 Insh Marshes

LOCATION Ten miles (16 km) south of Aviemore and 6 miles (10 km) north of Kingussie on the B970 south of Insh. *Landranger Sheet 35, 775998.*

This RSPB Reserve comprises the largest tract of natural fen in northern Britain, forming part of the flood plain of the River Spey. Apart from the extensive tracts of sedge fen, areas of shallow standing water are bordered by reed-beds with stands of willow, alder and bird cherry by the river. On higher ground, there is birch woodland with an understorey of juniper scrub. The woodland supports a few pairs of pied flycatcher, a rare breeding species in Scotland.

Highlights
Wintering **whooper swans.**

Time and season
Winter for **swans,** autumn for passage waders and raptors, spring and summer for a wide range of marsh and woodland birds. All year: **mallard, shoveler, tufted duck, buzzard, marsh harrier.** Winter: **whooper swan, wigeon, goldeneye,** goosander, **red-breasted merganser.** Summer: **water rail,** spotted crake (rare), **lapwing, curlew, common sandpiper, black-headed gull, redstart, grasshopper warbler, sedge warbler, willow warbler, meadow pipit, tree pipit, redpoll.**

GRAMPIAN

53 Loch of Strathbeg

LOCATION Between Peterhead and Fraserburgh; leave A952 east on an unclassified road between Blackhill and Crimond. *Landranger Sheet 30, 073590.*

An RSPB Reserve of over 2,300 acres; one of the most important haunts for waterfowl in Britain. The focus of the Reserve is the 2-mile (3.2-km) loch, actually a large dune slack pool, separated from the sea by a wide sand-and-gravel bar. Freshwater marsh to the west of the Loch and fen woodland in the south-west corner add to the diversity of wetland habitats.

Highlights
Autumn roost for up to 2,000 **greylag** and pink-footed **geese,** and some 600 **whooper swans.**

Time and season
Varied winter wildfowl population and important in autumn as a staging post for **ducks** and **geese** on migration to and from Iceland and Scandinavia. Winter: **whooper swan, greylag goose, mallard, wigeon, pochard, tufted duck, goldeneye,** goosander, **greylag goose,** pink-footed goose, **whooper swan.** Summer: **great crested grebe,** eider. Passage: **mute swan, marsh harrier,** green sandpiper.

ULSTER

CO DOWN

54 Castle Ward

LOCATION **On the southern shore of Strangford Lough, 7 miles (11 km) north-east of Downpatrick, one-and-a-half miles (2.5 km) west of Strangford village, entrance by Ballycutter Lodge. J 752494.**

An attractive estate of nearly 800 acres. Apart from the parkland surrounding the house and its adjacent woodland, the estate includes several ponds, stretches of mudflat, bog, and farmland. The adjacent areas of Strangford Lough are interesting in winter for waders and water birds such as **heron,** turnstone and **greenshank.** The woodland area has breeding sparrowhawk.

Highlights
Birds of water, farm and woodland.

Time and season
All year: **little grebe, buzzard, kestrel, woodcock, barn owl, long-eared owl, kingfisher, goldcrest, yellowhammer.** Summer: **sedge warbler, willow warbler,** chiffchaff, spotted flycatcher.

CO FERMANAGH

55 Castlecaldwell

LOCATION **Five miles (8 km) east of Belleek on the main Belleek to Kesh road in West Fermanagh. H007603.**

Situated on the extreme north-western bank of Lower Lough Erne, this RSPB Reserve covers nearly 600 acres of commercial forest, together with the waters of the Lough and its indented shoreline which has been colonised by scrub over the last 100 years producing varied nesting sites. The Reserve also includes some 20 islands and the RSPB owns or manages a further 13, all on Lower Lough Erne.

Breeding woodland species include sparrowhawk, and siskin. Information centre and nature trail.

Highlights
Prime site for both wetland and woodland birds. Main breeding location for common scoter in Britain with 100-120 pairs.

Time and season
Spring and early summer. Summer: **great crested grebe, little grebe, heron, mallard, teal, tufted duck,** corncrake (in nearby meadows), **black-headed gull, grasshopper warbler, sedge warbler, willow warbler,** chiffchaff.

56 and 57 Lough Neagh and Lough Beg

LOCATION **Lying some 20 miles (32 km) west of Belfast, Lough Neagh is the largest freshwater lake in Britain and includes the boundaries of four counties. Lough Beg forms a mere, just one-and-a-quarter miles (2 km) to the north on the River Bann. D3037 and D298395.**

Both Loughs are extremely rich in habitats including islands and extensive reed-fringed shallows, especially along the southern shore of Lough Neagh at Lurgan. In addition, Lough Beg has a winter flood area on its western side which expands existing areas of permanent water. There are also flooded sand-pits at its southern end, overgrown in parts with tangles of brambles, shrubs and small trees. Lough Beg is a particularly attractive site for passage waders including North American dowitcher and buff-breasted sandpiper.

Highlights
Winter wildfowl and passage migrants; large populations of breeding **great crested grebe** and **tufted duck.**

Time and season
All year: **great crested grebe.** Winter: **teal, pintail, shoveler, tufted duck, pochard, goldeneye, red-breasted merganser, Bewick's swan, whooper swan.**

REPUBLIC OF IRELAND

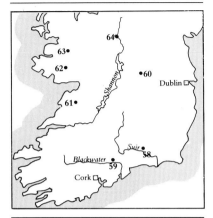

CO WATERFORD

58 Coolfin Marshes

Wet meadowland and marsh beside the River Suir near Portlaw, overwintering ground for some 200 **greylag geese** as well as **ducks** and **swans.** Access from L26 at junction for Portlaw.

59 Lismore Callows

Wet meadowland beside River Blackwater; flooding attracts good numbers of **wigeon** and **black-tailed godwit** with smaller numbers of other **ducks** and **swans.** Situated beside T30 about 3 miles (5 km) west of Lismore.

CO WESTMEATH

60 Westmeath Lakes

A complex of shallow lakes on limestone. The most interesting are Derravargh: diving **ducks,** particularly **pochard** (6,000) in autumn and **coot** (3,000); Owel: up to 2,000 **shoveler** each winter; Iron: winter flock of up to 200 **white-fronted geese.** Access by minor roads and tracks.

CO CLARE

61 Ballyallia Lake

A small shallow lake of some 90 acres with high concentrations of winter wildfowl including **wigeon** (3,000), **shoveler** (500) and **gadwall** (180). Also breeding site of **great crested grebe.** Access off T11 about 2 miles (3 km) north of Ennis.

CO GALLOWAY

62 Lough Corrib

Large lake 22 miles (35.5 km) long divided into two main basins with extensive marshland at southern end. Up to 22,000 **pochard** and 11,000 **coot** overwinter mainly on southern basin. Also large population of breeding gulls on numerous islands. Access off T40 and T77, then along minor roads.

CO MAYO

63 Lough Carra

Large extremely shallow lake on limestone with surrounding reed-beds. Large breeding populations of **mallard** and **black-headed gulls.** Winter visitors include high numbers of both **mallard** and **shoveler.** T40 passes west of the lake.

64 River Shannon

The River flows through several lakes before entering the head of the estuary at Limerick City. Important flooded areas for wildfowl lie between Portumna and Lanesborough, including the Rivers Suck and Brosna. Best single area is at the junction of the Little Brosna River with the Shannon, south of Banagher with up to 14,000 **wigeon** and 2,000 **black-tailed godwit** in the spring and 2,000 **teal** and 300 **white-fronted geese** in winter.

Understanding birds

It is a bird's feathers that make it unique. There are other animals which fly, sing, make nests, lay eggs or migrate. But only birds have feathers. The nearest any other creature comes to having feathers is the reptile with its scales. Feathers probably evolved from scales, and birds and reptiles such as crocodiles and dinosaurs, for all their immense differences, shared a common ancestor.

Scientists are unable to tell exactly how the change from scales to feathers took place. Fossils of *Archaeopteryx,* the first known bird, shows that 150 million years ago feathers were already the same as they are today. But *Archaeopteryx* was no ordinary bird. Although it had feathers, it still had the teeth and long, bony tail of a reptile. Its breastbone was poorly developed and lacked the deep keel to which the flight muscles of modern birds are anchored. This suggests that at best it could only flap its wings weakly. Probably it relied mostly on gliding.

Their mastery of the air is the main reason why birds have been one of nature's most spectacular successes, evolving into thousands of different species and colonising every corner of the globe. In every aspect of their physiology, they reveal how perfectly they are adapted for flight. Some bones which were separate in their flightless ancestors – including bones in the wings and sections of the backbone – are now fused together, giving greater strength. Others are hollow and strutted, combining strength with lightness. Massive breast muscles power their wings, while their hearts keep pace with their intense energy, beating with fantastic rapidity;

in the case of a robin's heart, for instance, more than eight times as fast as a man's. Birds' eyesight is also the most acute in the animal world, adapted to gathering information at the same high speed at which they live.

Speed, infinite mobility and wildness: these are the characteristics common to all bird-life, which make birds so fascinating to watch. Birds rarely remain still, except when they are roosting or incubating their eggs, and they are always on the alert. But their actions are never without meaning; every movement a bird makes has an exact purpose. One of the greatest satisfactions in bird-watching is understanding why birds behave as they do – learning to tell the difference between threat and courtship displays, for instance, or observing how they look after their feathers or build their nests.

Bird classification

It is now established that there are some 8,600 different kinds of birds in the world. At one time the number was put as high as 25,000, partly because the same bird had different names in different parts of the world. This was before the modern system of classification had been developed, which groups birds according to their evolutionary relationship with one another, and gives each of them a set of scientific names.

The basic unit of the modern system is the species, an interbreeding group of identical birds. The next, larger division is the genus, a group of closely related species of birds, usually showing obvious similarities. The black-headed gull, for instance, is one of many species belonging to the gull genus. A bird's

scientific name always states the genus first, then the species. The black-headed gull is called *Larus ridibundus* – translated literally, the name means 'Gull, laughing'.

When one genus closely resembles another, they are grouped together to make a family. Gulls are similar in many ways to terns, and both belong to the family *Laridae,* named after Greek word for a gull; in some schemes of classification they are separated into sub-families, *Larinae* (gulls) and *Sterninae* (terns). The families are grouped into 27 different orders. The family of gulls and terns belongs, together with a great variety of other sea and shore birds, in the order *Charadriiformes,* after the Greek for 'plover'. All the orders together make up the zoological class *Aves* – 'Birds'.

Keeping records

To become a really proficient birdwatcher, it is important to keep a field notebook, such as this one, and to keep a logbook at home in which to write up your notes in greater detail. Your notebooks will soon become an invaluable fund of knowledge.

At the end of each year, check through your notes to see if they are worth sending to the records committee of your local bird-watching society. The annual bird reports of these societies, combined on a national level, often form the basis on which ornithologists establish the current status of a species.

Taking part in a census

Once you have become experienced at

bird-watching you may wish to take part in a detailed census, organised at a local or national level. A census can take the form of a monthly count of birds at a reservoir or estuary, to check on the numbers of wildfowl or waders, for instance; or in the spring and summer months it may entail finding out the breeding population of a particular area. One such census is the Nest Record Scheme, co-ordinated by the British Trust for Ornithology, which aims to establish the exact breeding status of all British birds. If you wish to join this scheme, contact the BTO at Beech Grove, Tring, Hertfordshire.

Alternatively, you may prefer to start your own project. This could take the form of a census of the birds seen in your garden at different times of the year, or you could study the change in the type and number of birds on land undergoing development. Bird populations are always fluctuating, and keeping track of the changes taking place around you can be a fascinating pastime.

Bird ringing

The method of catching birds and ringing them – putting a light metal band on one leg – has been in use since the end of the nineteenth century, as a way of studying bird behaviour and migrations and to help in the conservation of particular species. Ringing birds has enabled conservationists to find out where certain species stop to rest while on migration; and international agreements between governments have made some of these stop-over points into nature reserves, to help to ensure the survival of the species.

The most common way of trapping birds in order to ring them is by using mist-nets – black nylon or terylene nets which are almost invisible to a bird in flight. The ringer quickly and carefully removes the trapped bird from the net, then fits the ring on its leg. The ring carried the address of the BTO, and a number which is unique to that bird. Before being released, the bird is identified and weighed and full details are taken of its age, sex and condition. The records are then sent for processing and storage to the BTO. If you wish to become a ringer yourself, you must be trained by a recognised expert and obtain a permit from the BTO. As co-ordinators of the ringing scheme the BTO will be able to supply any information which you may require.

If you ever find a dead, ringed bird, remove the ring and send it to the BTO, with details about when and where you found the bird and, if you can tell, what may have caused its death. They will then send you all the information gathered about the bird when it was originally ringed. Never attempt to remove a ring from the leg of a living bird, as birds' bones are very fragile and can easily be broken.

Photographing birds

Bird photography requires great patience, as well as expensive equipment and considerable technical skill; but, if you can afford it, it is one of the most satisfying activities that an amateur bird-watcher can perform.

The most suitable camera is a single-lens reflex camera, with interchangeable lenses and a through-the-lens metering system. At least one telephoto lens of not less than 200 mm focal length is essential; this will enable you to photograph birds in close-up without alarming them. A tripod and cable release will help to eliminate blurred pictures caused by camera shake.

Remember how easily birds can be disturbed, and never do anything which threatens their welfare. Disturbing birds in the breeding season often causes them to desert their eggs or young, and for certain species the law requires that you have a licence before photographing them at the nest. The Royal Society for the Protection of Birds publishes a booklet, *Wild Birds and the Law,* which lists all the protected species.

Many species of birds are heard more often than they are seen, and in recent years recording bird-song has become an increasingly popular hobby among bird-watchers. As with photography, it is necessary to choose your equipment with great care, and preferably with expert guidance; but even with inexpensive tape-recorders it is possible to achieve many interesting results.

Societies and journals

The best way to make contact with other bird-watchers is to join your local bird-watching society. These societies often organise weekend excursions to nature reserves and sanctuaries, and also have occasional films and lectures presented by experts. These meetings are excellent opportunities to discuss any problems you may have with bird identification or understanding individual bird behaviour, as well as for gaining advice on the purchase of equipment. The annual bird reports which they publish will give you much useful information about the birds in your own area. Most public libraries can tell you the addresses of local societies, and how to join them.

There are also several national ornithological societies, some of which you may wish to join. The major societies are listed below, together with a selection of their journals about bird-watching.

BRITISH ORNITHOLOGISTS' UNION *c/o The Zoological Society of London, Regent's Park, London NW1 4RY.* One of the world's foremost ornithological societies, chiefly for professional ornithologists, or advanced amateurs. It holds occasional meetings, with lectures or films on any aspect of world ornithology. Publishes *Ibis,* a quarterly journal which contains articles covering a wide range of subjects related to birds.

BRITISH TRUST FOR ORNITHOLOGY *Beech Grove, Station Road, Tring, Hertfordshire.* Similar to the BOU, but deals solely with British birds. Runs the national ringing scheme, the Common Birds Census, and various other educational or research projects. Publishes the journal *Bird Study.*

IRISH WILDBIRD CONSERVANCY *Southview, Church Road, Greystones, Co. Wicklow, Ireland.* The Irish equivalent of the BTO.

ROYAL SOCIETY FOR THE PROTECTION OF BIRDS *The Lodge, Sandy, Bedfordshire.* Owns and manages some of the most important nature reserves in Britain. Runs courses for beginners in many parts of the country, and publishes *Birds,* a quarterly magazine dealing with all aspects of bird-watching.

SCOTTISH ORNITHOLOGISTS CLUB *21 Regent Terrace, Edinburgh, Scotland.* Similar aims to the BTO, with particular reference to bird-watching and birdlife in Scotland.

THE WILDFOWL TRUST *Slimbridge, Gloucestershire.* Mainly concerned with the conservation of wildfowl. Manages several important sanctuaries where wild ducks, geese and swans can be observed at close quarters. Publishes *Wildfowl,* an annual report containing articles about wildfowl, and information about the Trust's collection.

ROYAL SOCIETY FOR NATURE CONSERVATION *The Green, Nettleham, Lincoln LN2 2NR.* Parent body of the Nature Conservation Trusts, which manage more than 1,300 reserves, many of which provide facilities for bird-watchers.

The bird-watcher's code

Whatever you choose to do as a bird-watcher – whether you prefer travelling widely to watch birds, or setting up a hide in one place, whether you are photographing, recording or counting birds – there is a code of conduct which should always be observed.

Never cause undue disturbance to birds, especially in the breeding season.
Always obtain permission before venturing on to private land.
Keep to paths as far as possible.
Never park so as to block the entrance to a field.
Leave gates as you find them.
Leave no litter.
When you have finished watching a bird, leave quietly in order not to frighten it.

Glossary

A

Accidental Uncommon visitor, arriving only when blown off course or disorientated; same as VAGRANT.

Adult Bird with fully developed final plumage.

Albino Bird with partial or total absence of dark pigment, giving it a white appearance. In a true albino, dark pigment is completely absent from the beak, eyes and legs, as well as from the plumage.

Axillaries Feathers in the axilla, or 'armpit'.

B

Barb Branch of the central shaft of a feather.

Barbule Branch of the BARB of a feather.

Bastard wing Group of feathers at first digit of wing from tip, or 'thumb'.

Blaze Coloured patch at base of bill.

Breeding plumage Plumage developed during the breeding season.

Brood patch Area of featherless, thickened skin on abdomen developed as an aid to incubating eggs.

C

Call Brief sound used for contact within a species, to warn of danger, and so on. Same throughout the year.

Carpal joint Forward-pointing joint of the wing when closed: the 'wrist'.

Cere Fleshy covering at base of bill found in hawks, pigeons and other birds. Often distinctively coloured.

Colony Gathering of some species of birds, to breed or roost.

Contour feathers Feathers lying along the body, streamlining it and insulating it against cold.

Coverts Feathers overlying the bases of the tail feathers or major wing feathers; for example tail covert, wing covert, under-wing covert. Also the area of feathers covering a bird's ear (ear covert).

Crepuscular Active only at dusk and dawn.

D

Dialect Local variation in the song of a bird population.

Display Posturing, usually by male bird to attract female during breeding season; also to warn off rival males, and to defend TERRITORY.

Diurnal Active only in daylight hours.

Dorsal Belonging to a bird's back.

Down First feather covering of young birds of some species.

E

Eclipse Post-breeding moult, characteristic of ducks, during which for a short time, males become flightless, lose their bright plumage and come to resemble females.

Egg-tooth Horny protuberance at tip of upper MANDIBLE of a chick, used to crack shell when emerging.

Eruption Mass movement of birds, occurring at irregular intervals.

Escape Species or individual bird escaped or liberated from captivity.

Exotic Term describing a species foreign to an area.

Eye-stripe Distinctively coloured stripe of feathers leading back from or through the eye.

F

Feral Term describing wild bird population that originated in captivity.

First year Period between the time a bird leaves the nest and the following breeding season.

Fore-edge, fore-wing Leading edge of wing.

G

Gape Angle of bill opening.

H

Hawking Capture of flying insects while bird is on the wing.

Hood Area of contrasting plumage covering most of head.

I

Immature Bird in plumage indicating lack of sexual maturity.

Introduced Term describing birds captured in one area and released in another.

Invasion Sudden mass arrival of birds not usually seen in an area.

J

Juvenile Bird in its first covering of true feathers.

L

Lek Place where males of some species, for example black grouse, display communally prior to breeding.

Lore Area between base of upper mandible and eye.

M

Mandible Upper or lower part of bill.
Mantle Back.
Melanistic Term describing a bird with an abnormally large amount of dark pigment in its plumage.
Migrant Species that does not remain on its breeding grounds all year.
Mob Aggression, usually directed by a number of birds against a predator.
Morph Same as PHASE.
Moustachial stripe Streak of contrasting feathers running back from the base of the bill.

N

Nail Shield or horny plate at tip of upper mandible, found in some geese and ducks.
Nidiculous Term describing young that are hatched helpless and blind, and stay in nest for a considerable time.
Nidifugous Term describing young that are hatched with eyes open, covered with down and able to leave nest almost immediately.
Nocturnal Active only during darkness.

O

Oceanic Another word for PELAGIC.
Orbital ring Fleshy ring around the eye.

P

Partial migrant Species of which some individuals migrate, but others remain on their breeding grounds.
Passage migrant Bird usually breeding and wintering outside an area, but regularly seen on migration.
Pelagic Term describing sea-bird that seldom or never visits land except in breeding season.
Phase Distinctive variation of plumage within a species.
Preen gland Gland on rump that exudes oil as an aid to preening.
Primary feathers A bird's main flight feathers, attached to 'hand'.

R

Race Term used to describe a subspecies of a bird which inhabits a different region and has slightly different physical characteristics, as for example, plumage pattern.
Raptor Bird of prey, excluding owls.
Resident Bird present throughout year.

S

Scapulars Feathers above the shoulders of a bird.
Secondary feathers Flight feathers attached to 'forearm'.
Sedentary Term describing species that does not migrate or move far from its breeding ground.
Song Language of a bird, intended to identify its TERRITORY to other birds and attract females to intended breeding area.
Speculum Contrasting patch of SECONDARY FEATHERS in wing, usually in ducks.
Spinning Action of some water birds, for example phalaropes, swimming in tight circles to bring food to the surface.

Stoop Term describing dive of a raptor, especially peregrine falcon.
Sub-song Subdued song outside period of full song, or by young males.
Subspecies See RACE.
Superciliary stripe Streak of contrasting feathers above a bird's eye.

T

Tarsus Part of a bird's leg from directly above the toes to the first joint.
Territory Part of a habitat defended by the bird or group of birds occupying it against other birds.

V

Vagrant Uncommon visitor, arriving only when blown off course or disorientated.
Ventral Belonging to a bird's underside or belly.

W

Wattles Fleshy protuberances on head.
Web Flesh between toes of water-birds.
Wing-bar Conspicuous stripe across the wing, formed by tips of feathers of contrasting colour.
Wing linings Under-wing COVERTS.
Winter plumage Plumage developed outside breeding season, by male or female bird.
Winter visitor Bird that usually breeds outside the area in which it is seen in winter.

Index

BIRDS

A
avocet 45

B
bittern 16
bunting, corn 93
  reed 95
buzzard 37

C
coot 43
cuckoo 56
curlew 53
  stone 44

D
dipper 75
diver, red-throated 12
duck, tufted 30

F
fieldfare 86

G
gadwall 25
garganey 27
godwit, black-tailed 52
goldcrest 81
goldeneye 33
goldfinch 90
goose, Canada 23
  greylag 20
  white fronted 21
grebe, great crested 14
  little 13
greenshank 49
gull, black-headed 55

H
harrier, hen 34
  marsh 35
  Montagu's 36
heron 15

K
kestrel 38
kingfisher 63

L
lapwing 46
linnet 92

M
mallard 26
martin, sand 64
merganser, red-breasted 32
moorhen 42

N
nightingale 87
nightjar 62

O
owl, barn 57
  little 58
  long-eared 60
  short-eared 59

P
partridge 39
  red-legged 40
pintail 29
pipit, meadow 69
  tree 68
pochard 31

R
rail, water 41
redpoll 91
redshank 54
redstart 85
redwing 88
reedling, bearded 89
rook 74
ruff 47

S
sandpiper, common 51
shoveler 28
shrike, red-backed 73
skylark 67
snipe 48
stonechat 83
swallow 65
swan, Bewick's 17
  mute 19
  whooper 18
swift 61

T
teal 24

W
wagtail, grey 72
  pied 71
  yellow 70
warbler, Dartford 78
  grasshopper 76
  sedge 77
  willow 80
wheatear 84
whinchat 82
whitethroat, lesser 79
wigeon 22
woodcock 50
woodlark 66

Y
yellowhammer 94

Index

SITES

A
Abberton Reservoir 108-9
Ashridge 108

B
Ballyallia Lake 119
Blickling 111
Boarstall Duck Decoy 105
Bramshaw Commons 102
Branscombe 99
Bransdale 113
Breinton Springs 105-6
Breydon Water 110
Brockhampton 106

C
Castlecaldwell 118
Castle Ward 118
Caudale 114
Chew Valley 101
Clumber Park 107-8
Coolfin Marshes 119

D
Danbury Common 108
Dovedale 106-7
Duddingston Loch 116
Dudmaston 106
Dunwich Heath 109

E
Erdigg 104

F
Failand 101
Fairburn Ings 112-13
Flanders Moss 116
Frensham Common 102-3

G
Godlingston Heath 100-1
Golden Cap Estate 99-100

H
Hardwick Hall 107
Hartland Moor 100
Hartsop 114
Hornsea Mere 112

Horsey Mere 110-11

I
Insh Marshes 117

K
Kinver Edge 106

L
Lake District 113
Lanhydrock 98-9
Leighton Moss 114
Lingwood Common 108
Lismore Callows 119
Llangorse Lake 104
Loch Leven 116
Loch Lomond 115-16
Loch of Kinnordy 117
Loch of Strathbeg 117
Lochwinnoch 115
Loe, The 98
Lough Beg 118
Lough Carra 119
Lough Corrib 119
Lough Neagh 118

M
Marazion Marsh 98
Middlebere Heath 100
Minsmere 109

O
Osterley Park 103
Ouse Washes 109

P
Petworth Park 102

R
Radipole Lake 100
Ryder's Down 104

S
Salcombe Regis 99
Sedgemoor, West 99
Shannon, River 119
Slimbridge 105
Stodmarsh 103
Studland 100-1

T
Tatton Park 111-12
Threave 115

W
Westmeath Lakes 119
Worsbrough Mill and Country
Park 112

Acknowledgements

The editor and publishers would like to thank the following for their invaluable help in compiling information for this book:

Katherine Hearn (Assistant Adviser on Conservation) and Keith Alexander (Surveyor, Biological Survey Team), The National Trust.

Richard Nairn, Director of the Irish Wild Bird Conservancy.

The British Trust for Ornithology, Tring, including local representatives.

The Berkshire, Bucks and Oxon Naturalists' Trust.

Jim Worgan, Warden, the Boarstall Duck Decoy.

Editorial and design
Researched, written and edited by David Black; assistant editor Rosemary Dawe; designed by Arthur Brown; map on page 96 by Eugene Fleury.

RIVER, WETLAND & LOWLAND BIRDS
is based on the Reader's Digest Field Guide to Birds of Britain to which the following made major contributions:

CONSULTANTS AND AUTHORS
Dr Philip J.K. Burton, British Museum (Natural History)
Robert Gillmor   Howard Ginn, M.A.
Wildlife Advisory Branch, Nature Conservancy Council
T.W. Parmenter
John Parslow, Director (Conservation), Royal Society for the Protection of Birds
Cyril A. Walker, British Museum (Natural History)
D.I.M. Wallace, B.A.

ARTISTS

Stephen Adams	Hermann Heinzel
Norman Arlott	Mick Loates
Peter Barrett	Sean Milne
Trevor Boyer	Robert Morton
John Busby	D.W. Ovenden
John Francis	Patrick Oxenham
Robert Gillmor	Jim Russell
Tim Hayward	Ken Wood

CARTOGRAPHY
The distribution maps were based on information supplied by John Parslow and prepared by Clyde Surveys Ltd